"As youn[g] ... ling, it's important to know wh... ig step. God uses the marital an... covenant. If you want to grow in ... ploring the Bible's rich teaching on this subject is an essential foundation. And with this well-informed and accessible introduction, you'll grow in your appreciation for our ever-faithful Triune God. It is a pleasure to commend such an outstanding resource."

Michael Horton, J. Gresham Machen Professor of Systematic Theology and Apologetics, Westminster Seminary California.

———————

"In *Faithful God*, Antonio Coppola provides a concise, clear, and Christ-centred introduction to the covenant bond between our Sovereign Creator-Redeemer and us, his (shamefully) unfaithful, yet still beloved people. This relationship shapes the Bible's history of redemption, and it unlocks the treasures of Scripture's multifaceted display of God's amazing, ever-faithful grace in Jesus. Read, learn, and worship in wonder."

Dennis E. Johnson, Professor Emeritus of Practical Theology, Westminster Seminary California; author, Walking with Jesus through His Word: Discovering Christ in All the Scriptures.

———————

"*Faithful God* is a welcome indigenous contribution to theological discourse in South Africa. Antonio Coppola provides a clear introduction to God's covenantal relationship to the church and the world. This refined confessional Reformed perspective is much needed in a context where conceptions of covenant and cultural engagement have threatened clarity on the gospel and the mission of the church."

Simon Jooste, Pastor of Reformed Church Southern Suburbs, Cape Town, South Africa.

"God's covenants with his people appear throughout the pages of holy writ, and thus any Bible-believing Christian should seek to survey, study, and soak in this truth. Antonio Coppola has written an accessible and brief introduction to help Christians understand this vital doctrine. Grounded in Scripture and clearly presented, *Faithful God: An Introduction to Covenant Theology* is an excellent place to begin studying God's covenants and a wonderful refresher for those already familiar with the topic."

J. V. Fesko, Harriet Barbour Professor of Systematic and Historical Theology, Reformed Theological Seminary, Jackson, Mississippi.

———————

"*Faithful God* contains sound biblical truths that are practical and useful. In the book, Antonio Coppola answers key questions regarding our identity in relation to God and his covenants. This book is timely, necessary and biblical."

Tiaan Jordaan, Pastor, Die Kruis, Pretoria, South Africa.

———————

"Reformed Theology is growing slowly but surely in Africa. The best way to understand it is by studying the covenants God made with his people throughout Scripture. In this book, Antonio Coppola makes it easier to do this. He paints a picture of the covenant God who not only is a covenant-keeping God, but who also creates a covenant people. He demonstrates how the covenants hold Old and New Testaments together and helps us make sense of God's covenant relationship with us. If you are new to Reformed theology and you want to understand how God relates to you and the church, this is your book."

Victor Nakah, International Director Africa, Mission to the World (MTW).

Faithful God

An Introduction to
Covenant Theology

Antonio Coppola

Lig in Duisternis
UITGEWERS

Cover Design:
Anneli de Beer

Published by:
First Edition: Die Boekuitgewers (dbu.boeke@gmail.com)
Print on Demand: Lig in Duisternis Uitgewers (www.liginduisternis.co.za)
E-book: Lig in Duisternis Uitgewers (www.liginduisternis.co.za)

Book ISBN: 978-0-6399675-6-1
E-book ISBN: 978-1-86855-277-1

Dedicated to:

the saints at

Covenant Waterfall Presbyterian Church

Contents

Acknowledgements 2

Foreword 3

Introduction 5

Chapter 1: The Covenant of Redemption 11

Chapter 2: The Covenant of Works 19

Chapter 3: The Covenant of Grace 28

Chapter 4: The Noahic Covenant 36

Chapter 5: The Abrahamic Covenant 46

Chapter 6: The Mosaic Covenant 55

Chapter 7: The Davidic Covenant 66

Chapter 8: The New Covenant 73

Conclusion 84

Bibliography 86

Acknowledgements

I am grateful to many friends, colleagues and mentors for the various roles that they played in helping me make this book a reality. I must express my deep gratitude to the faculty of my alma mater, Westminster Seminary California, and to the pastors of New Life Presbyterian Church, Escondido (PCA), where I was a member for three years. My life and faith were enriched immeasurably as a result of the time spent under their teaching and pastoral care while I lived in California. It was they who introduced me to the wonders of covenant theology and in so doing opened up for me a whole new exciting world. Covenant theology has enriched my faith in Christ, my grasp of the gospel, deepened my understanding of the story of the Scriptures and pointed me increasingly to our faithful God who always keeps his promises. This is what has motivated me to write this book, that you too would be encouraged and grown in your faith in our faithful God and Saviour Jesus Christ and better grasp the glories of the gospel.

In particular, I wish to thank two of my Westminster professors, Dennis Johnson and David VanDrunen, as well as Simon Jooste, for taking the time to read through my draft and offer me much constructive feedback. I am deeply grateful for their input and suggestions, which have gone a long way in shaping the final product.

I am grateful for my friends and colleagues at Mukhanyo Theological College, Brian DeVries, Anneke Viljoen, Ashley Govender and Bongile Ntiwane, who all encouraged me throughout the writing process. Thank you also to my cousin, Marina Johnson, for kindly editing my manuscript. I am also thankful to Douwe Drijfhout from the Vrye Gereformeerde Kerke in Suid-Afrika for seeing potential in my first manuscript and initiating the process for publication. And to my parents, Ginette and Mino Coppola, who have always loved me and supported me through thick and thin.

Most of all I am thankful to my God, the one and only God: Father, Son and Holy Spirit, for his steadfast love and undeserving grace to me, and his continued faithfulness in spite of my faithlessness (2 Tim. 2:13).

Foreword

It was in seminary when I first learned about covenant theology. In one of our first modules, Old Testament Theology, we traced the story of God's covenant promise from the first pages of the Bible, through the Old Testament history of redemption, and to its fulfilment in the person and work of Christ.

This story of God's covenant was a wonderful treat for me! I had grown up in a faithful Bible-believing church; from a child I was taught the stories and doctrines of God's precious Word. But covenant theology brought all these stories and doctrines together into a beautiful big-picture perspective like never before.

Learning covenant theology was a wonderful surprise, not because it taught me new truth, but rather because it brought the same old story to life again, in new perspective for me. The same Old Testament stories, which I knew so well, had much broader meaning as the covenantal framework gave me a timeline within which to organise these stories, according to the Spirit's inspired structure. The thread of the unfolding gospel promise, woven throughout the Old Testament and fully displayed in the New Testament, was much easier to trace as we studied it in light of God's gracious dealing with his covenant people.

Covenant theology is God's inspired framework that helps us understand his Word better. It helped me see the highpoints in the history of redemption, which in turn highlighted for me the deep and rich Old Testament doctrines that all pointed to Christ and made his work in the New Testament appear much more glorious. Thus covenant theology gave me a new perspective of and appreciation for God's story, the history of redemption.

This book will do the same for you. The subtitle – An Introduction to Covenant Theology – describes the content, while the title hints strongly at the purpose: giving glory to our faithful God. It is organised chronologically, working from the first pages of Scripture to the later Old

Testament prophets who clearly anticipated the coming of Christ. And it presents covenant theology systematically in thoughtful ways, including practical reflection in each section to help the reader apply these truths.

I trust you will be blessed by this short introduction to a very important topic. I also hope this book motivates you to study covenant theology further and deeper. Learning covenant theology has helped me preach and teach the whole Bible – both Old and New Testaments – more faithfully with greater depth and richness. But even more importantly, covenant theology has helped me know God better, to think his thoughts after him and to practice his covenant love (Jer. 9:23-24).

My hope is that covenant theology will do the same for you. I hope and pray that this book helps you to know God more fully, to understand his Word more deeply, and to explain God's story to others more accurately.

Brian A. DeVries
Principal, Mukhanyo Theological College, South Africa
Good Friday 2022

Introduction

All of us will experience the pain of broken promises at some point in our lives. Whether it is disappointment and hurt when a trusted friend betrays our confidence, or the devastation of adultery in a marriage; we know what it is like to have promises broken. In fact much of our lives are characterised by broken promises: from the empty words of politicians to the lies we often read and hear in the media. Being true to one's word these days is a rare quality.

In the midst of the myriad of broken promises we face in this sinful world, God is the only One who truly and perfectly keeps his promises all of the time. Because he is infinitely good, he is faithful and true to all his promises. In fact, the Hebrew word, *'ĕmĕt*, which is often translated as "faithfulness" in the Old Testament, also means "truth". Faithfulness and truth are therefore inextricably connected. God is faithful to his promises, because his promises are true. God does not lie, therefore he is always true to his Word.

God is not only faithful and true in an abstract sense, but he is faithful and true to us as his own people. How is this so? God expresses his faithfulness to us through covenants that he makes with his people. This brings us to the heart of what this book is about: the covenants that God has made with his people in Scripture.

What then do we mean by "covenant"? Simply put, a covenant is a promise with obligations. God's covenants with us contain the nature of his promise to be our God and we his own people. In the covenants in the Bible, God makes unbreakable promises to be faithful to his people. His people are to respond to his promises through covenantal obligations. From God's covenants with Adam to Noah, and Abraham to Moses and David in the Old Testament, through to the New Covenant in Jesus Christ – we see God's faithfulness expressed. It is for this reason that the theme of this book is that God expresses his faithfulness to his people through his covenants. In order to unpack this, we are going to examine all the major covenants that God has made in the Scriptures through the course of this book.

Why are covenants relevant to us?

Our relationship with God is covenantal

Covenants are the way in which God relates to his people. Our relationship with God is not something that happens in isolation. Describing our relationship with God as our "personal relationship with Jesus" while not untrue, misses the covenantal dimension of our relationship with God. We do not have an unmediated, unregulated, free-for-all relationship with God. Our relationship with God is founded on terms set by him, not us. This is why understanding the nature of God's covenants with us is so important. It helps us better understand our relationship with God – how he has chosen to relate to us, and how we ought to respond in that relationship. One of the main aims of this book is to understand the nature of our relationship with God better. Surely this should be one of the most important things to want to do as a Christian?

Understanding covenants helps us understand what the Bible is about

It is easy to lose sight of the bigger picture when looking at the Bible. We often read portions of Scripture in isolation of the grander scheme of things and thus potentially miss the point of certain passages and misinterpret Scripture. The reality is that the Bible is structured around covenants. Covenants hold Scripture together. God has consistently dealt with his people throughout history through covenants. Therefore to really understand what Scripture is about, we need to understand how God's covenants work.

What then is Scripture really about? From Genesis to Revelation, the Bible is about Jesus Christ and his gospel. It is this that lies at the heart of the covenants in Scripture – who our God is, and how he has saved a people for himself in Christ. Understanding the beauty, majesty and grace of God in Christ through his gospel promises, is the primary reason that we need to understand the nature of his covenants.

Another reason why studying God's covenants is so important is that it helps us better divide the word of truth (2 Tim. 2:15). Having a covenantal framework to interpret Scripture helps us see how the Old and New Testaments relate to each other, the continuities and discontinuities between the two, and a healthy distinction between law and gospel. All of these things help us steer clear from many pitfalls and confusion when it comes to interpreting the Bible.

Covenant as Promise

It has already been asserted that a covenant is a promise. What then is the nature of this promise? A covenant is a relationship of oaths and bonds founded on mutual, though not necessarily equal commitments.[1] A covenant with which we are all familiar is marriage. It is a promise between a husband and wife, a lifelong commitment to each other that they will give themselves to each other, stay together for the rest of their lives, "to have and to hold, from this day forward, for better or for worse, for richer or for poorer, in sickness and in health, to love and to cherish, till death us do part, according to God's holy law, and this is my solemn vow."[2]

It is a promise made by two parties – both commit to upholding a set of promises. It defines the nature of the relationship. The framework of the relationship is legal. Law and relationship are not mutually exclusive. Marriage is fundamentally relational, yet it is also a legal institution, defined by God's law and recognised by the law of the land. It is the same with biblical covenants, as marriage is a covenant.

Biblical covenants, like the covenant of marriage, have common features:

Oath: The covenant involves making a commitment to doing certain things. For example, God made an oath with Abraham that he will give his descendants the Promised Land (Gen. 15:18-21). Likewise, in Exodus 24, Israel promised to obey all the commands that Moses read to them. They were sprinkled with blood, symbolising the death that would follow if they were to break their oath.

---

1 Michael Horton, *Introducing Covenant Theology* (Grand Rapids: Baker Books, 2006), 10.

2 *An Anglican Prayer Book*, 1989, Church of the Province of Southern Africa (Cape Town: Collins, 1989), 464.

Obligation: The covenant will always involve an obligation from both parties. The nature of the obligation depends on the covenant. Some biblical covenants are unilateral, for example, the covenant of grace. God promises to save his people. The promise of God is entirely his doing; he does all the saving work himself. How do those being saved respond to this? Nothing they do can earn the gift, their only obligation is to receive it as a gift of grace by faith, which leads to repentance. Yet other covenants in the Bible are bilateral. God promises to do something, only if his people do something in return. For example, in the covenant of works, God promises to bless his people only if his people obey him. Similarly, God promises to curse his people, if they disobey him.

Signs: Signs or symbols are used to represent the covenant. As a wedding ring symbolises a marriage covenant, so biblical covenants also have signs. For example, the rainbow is the sign of the Noahic covenant, circumcision is the sign of the Abrahamic covenant, and baptism and the Lord's Supper are the signs of the new covenant.

Covenant formula: In most biblical covenants, a pronouncement is made at the initiation of the covenant. As with marriage vows, God makes vows, or covenant formulas, for each covenant. The key covenant formula we see throughout Scripture is, "I will be your God and you will be my people" (Ex. 6:7, Lev. 26:12, Jer. 30:22, Ezek. 36:28, Rev. 21:3).

Ultimately, by understanding the various covenants in Scripture, we are pointed increasingly to our great God and Saviour Jesus Christ. What we shall see is through these covenants, God shows himself to be the One who is faithful, good, loving, holy and entirely trustworthy. He has covenanted to never break his promises to us, that we will be his people and he our faithful God forever.

Covenant Theology

Trying to understand the significance of the various covenants in Scripture is nothing novel. Christians have been doing this for two millennia. This book only stands upon the shoulders of many others who have engaged in what is known as "covenant theology." What then is covenant theology? It is an approach to theology, which, as Ligon Duncan says, "identifies the covenants as the fundamental organizing principle for the Bible's theology."[3] Traditionally, covenant theology has been associated with Reformed theology, i.e. the theology that emerged out of the Protestant Reformation of the sixteenth century. Indeed, Reformed theology is at its heart covenantal, and covenant theology most certainly developed and matured through the Reformation. In many ways, Reformed theology *is* covenant theology. The magisterial Reformers such as Martin Luther (1483-1546), Huldrych Zwingli (1484-1531), Heinrich Bullinger (1504-1575) and John Calvin (1509-1564) all identified the importance of how God relates to his people through covenants.[4] Further, the Reformed confessions of faith, especially the Westminster Standards (1647), are explicitly covenantal. Covenant theology was also taught by continental Reformed theologians, such as Zacharias Ursinus (1534-1583) and Caspar Olevianus (1536-1587), who co-authored the Heidelberg Catechism (1563), Francis Turretin (1623-1683) and Herman Witsius (1636-1708). There were also many English Puritans like William Perkins (1558-1602), Thomas Goodwin (1600-1680) and John Owen (1616-1683) who taught covenant theology.

While covenant theology is today strongly associated with Reformed theology, it was not invented by the Reformers. Instead the foundations for covenant theology had already been laid during the early and medieval church periods.[5] Church Fathers such as Irenaeus (130-202) and Tertullian (155-220) were both covenantal in their writings. And ultimately the apostles wrote about the idea of covenant throughout the New Testament, showing that covenantal thought was deeply rooted in the apostolic era.[6]

---

[3] Ligon Duncan, 'Foreword' in *Covenant Theology: Biblical, Theological, and Historical Perspectives*, eds. Guy Prentiss Waters, J. Nicholas Reid, and John R. Muether (Wheaton: Crossway, 2020), 24.

[4] Howard Griffith, 'Covenant in Reformation Theology' in *Covenant Theology: Biblical, Theological, and Historical Perspectives*, eds. Guy Prentiss Waters, J. Nicholas Reid, and John R. Muether (Wheaton: Crossway, 2020), 328-334.

[5] Michael G. Brown, 'The Covenantal Foundation of the Heidelberg Catechism' in *Puritan Reformed Journal* 7, 1 (2015), 89.

[6] Ligon Duncan, 'Covenant in the Early Church' in *Covenant Theology: Biblical, Theological, and Historical Perspectives*, eds. Guy Prentiss Waters, J. Nicholas Reid, and John R. Muether (Wheaton: Crossway, 2020), 294-308.

This book seeks to provide an introduction to historic Reformed covenant theology. Though there are certainly nuances within this stream, broadly speaking, covenant theology has historically taught that biblical history is the outworking of two covenants. The first covenant is the covenant of works, that God made with Adam before the fall. The second is the covenant of grace made after the fall. The various covenants in the Old Testament, God's covenants with Noah, Abraham, Moses and David, while distinct, are all expressions of the one covenant of grace.[7] What they all share in common is that they reveal God's plan of salvation, which culminates in the coming of Jesus Christ and the new covenant which he establishes.[8]

Let us now begin our journey through these covenants that we find in Scripture.

Discussion Questions

1. Explain the connection between God's faithfulness and truth. How is this expressed in his covenant promises to us?
2. Why is it important for us to understand our relationship to God as covenantal?
3. Why should we take the covenants in the Bible seriously? How do they help us in better understanding the message of Scripture?
4. Explain the different features of covenants.
5. What is "covenant theology"? Broadly speaking, how has it been explained historically in the church?

---

[7] I include the covenant of redemption as a pre-temporal expression of the covenant of grace (see chapter 1).

[8] J.V. Fesko, *The Theology of the Westminster Standards: Historical Context & Theological Insights* (Wheaton: Crossway, 2014), 127-137; Vern S. Poythress, *Theophany: A Biblical Theology of God's Appearing* (Wheaton: Crossway, 2018), 25.

1 | The Covenant of Redemption

Setting the Scene

Before God spoke the universe into being through the power of his Word, indeed, before the heavens and the earth existed, God was. Eternal, infinite and self-existent, without a beginning or end, the one and only true God: Father, Son and Holy Spirit, was always. And it was in eternity, that the Triune God established the very first covenant. This covenant is God's blueprint for our salvation, the eternal foundation and prototype of the covenant of grace. As any building has to be designed beforehand by an architect, so our redemption in Christ was planned before time by God.[9]

Before the creation of the world, God already had made a plan to send his Son to earth as the last Adam to deal with the sin of the first Adam. God did not choose to send Jesus to earth as a backup plan. Adam's fall into sin, and mankind's subsequent separation from God, did not take God by surprise. God's plan to send Jesus to earth to save his people was made before time, and it was always God's original plan. This original plan for the salvation of God's people was in form of a covenant, known as the covenant of redemption, or *pactum salutis* (pact of salvation).

What is the Covenant of Redemption?

It is a covenant among the Persons of the Trinity

All other covenants in Scripture are made between God and man. Not so with the covenant of redemption. This covenant was made among the Persons of the Godhead – the Father, Son and Holy Spirit. The purpose of the covenant is the redemption of God's people. The Father chose a people for himself. He then sent his Son Jesus to earth to save this people. He lived an obedient life in accordance with God's law, and died on the cross and rose again to life. The Father promised this people and a kingdom as a reward to his Son, and then sent his Holy Spirit to seal his people and to

---

[9] Louis Berkhof, *Systematic Theology* (Edinburgh: Banner of Truth, 1949), 270-271.

apply to us what was earned by the Son, uniting us with himself forever and giving us the promise that we would be raised again to life on the last day.[10]

It is a Covenant made Before Time

As we shall see in the coming chapters, every other covenant was made in time. The covenant of redemption, however, was made outside of time. It was made before the creation of the universe, when only the Trinity existed. The Godhead covenanted before anything existed, before the creation of the universe, that he would save us.

Though not explicitly calling it a covenant, the Westminster Confession of Faith, one of the historic Reformed confessions, in chapter 8.1, alludes to the covenant of redemption in the following manner:

> *It pleased God, in his eternal purpose, to choose and ordain the Lord Jesus, his only begotten Son, to be the Mediator between God and man, the Prophet, Priest, and King, the Head and Saviour of his church, the Heir of all things, and Judge of the world: unto whom he did from all eternity give a people, to be his seed, and to be by him in time redeemed, called, justified, sanctified, and glorified.*

What we can see from the confession is the affirmation that God ordained the salvation of his church through Christ in eternity. This is essentially the heart of the covenant of redemption.

Biblical Evidence for the Covenant of Redemption

Where then do we find evidence of this covenant in Scripture? Though there is evidence throughout the Bible, below are some key Scriptures that speak of the covenant.

Psalm 110

Psalm 110 is a messianic psalm, written by David. It describes the "LORD" (Hebrew = Yahweh) speaking to "my Lord" (Hebrew = Adonai) (110:1). The New Testament reveals that "my Lord" in this psalm is referring to God's promised Messiah, the son of David (Matt. 22:41-45, Mark 12:35-37, Luke 20:41-44, Acts 2:34-36, Heb. 7). Psalm 110 therefore describes an

---

10 Michael G. Brown & Zach Keele, *Sacred Bond: Covenant Theology Explored* (San Diego: Reformed Fellowship, 2012), 24; Berkhof, *Systematic Theology*, 269-270.

interaction between God the Father (Yahweh) and God the Son (Adonai). In this interaction, God the Father swears an oath to God the Son. This is described in verse 4, "The LORD has sworn and will not change his mind, "You are a priest for ever after the order of Melchizedek."

What is the significance of this oath? As we saw in the Introduction, an oath is a feature of a covenant. Psalm 110 is clearly using covenantal language. The nature of God the Father's covenant oath is that God the Son will be a priest in the order of Melchizedek. Melchizedek was the mysterious priest-king who met Abram in Genesis 14:17-24. Hebrews 7:7 describes him as being "without father or mother or genealogy, having neither beginning of days nor end of life, but resembling the Son of God he continues as a priest forever."

The Father appointed the Son as a mediator, a priest, between him and his chosen people in the order of Melchizedek. Hebrews 7 explains that this is so because Jesus was not born of the tribe of Levi, the priestly tribe of Israel, but of Judah. Because of the imperfection of the Levite priesthood in the light of the new covenant, Jesus' priesthood is not of Levi. God instead appointed his Son to the everlasting and perfect priesthood of Melchizedek through an oath (Heb. 7:28). Jesus was therefore appointed by his Father as the Great High Priest of his elect, a perfect mediator and intercessor between God and his people. When was this oath made? It was not made during Jesus' earthly ministry, nor was it made during the Old Testament period (Psalm 110 merely describes something that has already happened). This oath was made in eternity, as part of the covenant of redemption.[11]

Isaiah 53

The Old Testament prophet Isaiah alludes to the covenant in his incredible messianic prophecy in chapter 53. Here he portrays the relationship between the Father and Son, with regard to the salvation of God's people, using covenantal language. The death and suffering of Jesus is foretold in this passage, but what we also see is Christ's obedience to the Father in his life and death. Verse 5 says, "But he was wounded for our transgressions; he was crushed for our iniquities; upon him was the chastisement that brought us

[11] J.V. Fesko, *The Trinity and the Covenant of Redemption* (Fearn: Christian Focus Publications, 2016), 101-104; Brown & Keele, *Sacred Bond*, 26-27.

peace, and with his stripes we are healed." It is clear from this that Jesus' obedience to the Father's will brought us salvation.

Further on verse 10 says that, "it was the will of the LORD to crush him..." The suffering of Christ was according to the Father's will. This clearly points to a predetermined plan between the Father and the Son that the Son would suffer for sinners in order to save his people. Verse 11 says that by Christ's obedience to the Father, many would "be accounted righteous." Jesus' obedience resulted in the Father counting us as righteous before him. There is therefore clear evidence in Isaiah 53 that the salvation of God's people was planned by God in advance, pointing to the truth of the covenant of redemption.[12]

John's Gospel

Turning to the New Testament, to John's Gospel in particular, we see that there are many places which point to the covenant of redemption. Consider the following texts: Chapter 4:34, "My food is to do the will of him who sent me and to accomplish his work." Chapter 5:30, "I can do nothing on my own... because I seek not my own will but the will of him who sent me." Chapter 5:36, "For the works that the Father has given me to accomplish, the very works that I am doing, bear witness about me that the Father has sent me..." All three verses very clearly demonstrate that Jesus came to earth in order to accomplish the very specific plan of God the Father. What was that plan? Accomplish redemption for his people by dying an atoning death for sins on the cross.

Similarly, chapter 6:37-40 says, "All that the Father gives me will come to me, and whoever comes to me I will never cast out. For I have come down from heaven, not to do my own will but the will of him who sent me. And this is the will of him who sent me, that I should lose nothing of all that he has given me." Because the Father and the Son covenanted before the creation of the world to save a people chosen by God, none of those people will be lost. Jesus' work of redemption will effectively secure their salvation, which was planned before time through this covenant.

---

[12] Brown & Keele, *Sacred Bond*, 27-28.

Just before Jesus' crucifixion, he prayed to his Father, in chapter 17:1-5:

> *Father, the hour has come; glorify your Son that the Son may glorify you, since you have given him authority over all flesh, to give eternal life to all whom you have given him... I glorified you on earth, having accomplished the work you gave me to do. And now, Father, glorify me in your own presence with the glory that I had with you before the world existed.*

In this prayer, Jesus prayed about the people he came to save, his church. His mission from the Father was to save them through his obedience and atoning death on the cross, which he accomplished. As he was dying on the cross, facing the wrath of God that we should have faced, he cried out, "It is finished" (John 19:30). What it is that Jesus finished? His mission from his Father, given him in eternity, to save a people for himself – the heart of the covenant of redemption.[13]

Ephesians 1

Probably one of the clearest texts in Scripture regarding the covenant of redemption is Ephesians 1:3-14:

> *Blessed be the God and Father of our Lord Jesus Christ, who has blessed us in Christ with every spiritual blessing in the heavenly places, even as he chose us in him before the foundation of the world, that we should be holy and blameless before him. In love he predestined us for adoption to himself as sons through Jesus Christ, according to the purpose of his will, to the praise of his glorious grace, with which he has blessed us in the Beloved. In him we have redemption through his blood, the forgiveness of our trespasses, according to the riches of his grace, which he lavished upon us, in all wisdom and insight making known to us the mystery of his will, according to his purpose, which he set forth in Christ as a plan for the fullness of time, to unite all things in him, things in heaven and things on earth. In him we have obtained an inheritance, having been predestined according to the purpose of him who works all things according to the counsel of his will, so that we who were the*

[13] Brown & Keele, *Sacred Bond*, 29-30.

> *first to hope in Christ might be to the praise of his glory. In him you also, when you heard the word of truth, the gospel of your salvation, and believed in him, were sealed with the promised Holy Spirit, who is the guarantee of our inheritance until we acquire possession of it, to the praise of his glory.*

It is clear from this that the redemption of God's people was decided by God prior to the creation of the world (1:4-5). All three persons of the Trinity are involved in the redemption of God's people (1:3-5, 13-14). God the Father sovereignly elected his people, his church before creation, predestining them to salvation (1:3-4). The Father then commissioned Jesus Christ in the fullness of time to secure our redemption through the shedding of his blood (1:5-10). God seals his people with his Holy Spirit, who is the guarantee of the salvation of God's people (1:13-14). He applies the benefits of Christ's salvation to us – raises us from the dead, breathes life into us, makes us holy, convicts us of sin, transforms us into Christ's likeness, grants us gifts in order to edify the church, gives us a taste of the powers of the age to come, and assurance that we will be raised again to life in Christ.[14]

Why is this Covenant important for us?

It shows us that God is sovereign

Nothing in this world is left to chance. Because God is sovereign, he ordains all things that come to pass.[15] The covenant of redemption shows us God sovereignly and unconditionally elected a people for himself, his church, before the world began. He chose his people, not through any merit of our own (as he did so before we were able to do anything good or bad), but purely because of his good pleasure. This means that our salvation is rooted in the gracious and loving choice of God alone. Our salvation was sovereignly planned and executed exclusively by God, Father, Son and Holy Spirit through the covenant of redemption. It therefore rests entirely and securely in God himself.[16]

---

[14] Fesko, *The Trinity and the Covenant of Redemption*, 110-117.

[15] Westminster Confession of Faith 3.1.

[16] Canons of Dort I.7; Westminster Confession of Faith 10.2; Herman Bavinck. *Reformed Dogmatics, vol. 3, Sin and Salvation in Christ,* ed. John Bolt, trans. John Vriend. (Grand Rapids: Baker Academic, 2008), 212-215.

It reveals the love of God

The covenant of redemption provides us with a wonderful glimpse of the perfect love that has always existed between the Father, Son and Holy Spirit. The Godhead has always been enjoying love between the Persons of the Trinity before anything was created.

The Father shows his love for the Son by giving him a reward: the church, of which he is its head (Col. 1:18). The Son's love for the Father is revealed in the way that he willingly, even joyfully obeys his will, to the point of death on a cross (Heb. 12:2). The Spirit's love for the Father and the Son is expressed by his pouring out of himself on the church and sealing God's people for everlasting redemption.

We were created only as a result of an overflow of the love that was already there, not out of some need from God to receive love from his creation. As a result, God chose to set his love on us not out of anything special in us – not our foreseen faith or works, but purely out of the abundance of his eternal love. He loved us while we were still his enemies (Rom. 5:8-10).

It gives us great assurance

The fact that God covenanted before the creation of the world to save us, is incredibly comforting and encouraging. If God himself has chosen us before creation, has come down to die on the cross for us in Christ and has sealed us with his Spirit, then nothing in heaven and on earth can separate us from his love, nor can we fall out of favour with God or lose our salvation. We are his, not because of anything special within us, but purely because he chose to set his love upon us. We did not decide to choose God, rather he chose us (John 15:16). Because our salvation is rooted in his choice of us, instead of our choice of him, we can be sure that he will never let us go.[17] We have been made right before God not because of our obedience, but because of Christ's obedience on our behalf.

The Heidelberg Catechism, Q & A 60 sums this up nicely:

> *Q. How are you righteous before God?*
>
> *A. Only by true faith in Jesus Christ. Even though my conscience accuses me of having grievously sinned against all God's commandments, of*

---

[17] Canons of Dort I.12; Westminster Confession of Faith 18.4.

never having kept any of them, and of still being inclined toward all evil, nevertheless, without any merit of my own, out of sheer grace, God grants and credits to me the perfect satisfaction, righteousness, and holiness of Christ, as if I had never sinned nor been a sinner, and as if I had been as perfectly obedient as Christ was obedient for me. All I need to do is accept this gift with a believing heart.

Conclusion

The covenant of redemption shows us that from beginning to end, God is the author of our salvation. Salvation indeed belongs to the Lord! (Jon. 2:9). He alone is the initiator of it. He alone accomplishes it through his Son and he alone brings it to completion through his Spirit. We actually play no part in our salvation. It is all from God, and because of this it is purely grace; that is good news for us. If we had anything to do with our salvation, in terms of our own worthiness, works or level of faith, it would not be good news, because none of us is good enough on our own before God. Neither would it be a gift of grace, as we would have had to earn it. The truth is that God does it all, and we only receive it as a gift of grace by faith in Christ alone.

Discussion Questions

1. Why is the covenant of redemption unique from the other covenants in Scripture?
2. Explain, using Scriptures, how our Triune God, Father, Son and Holy Spirit, covenanted to save us?
3. Explain the unique role of each Person of the Trinity in achieving our salvation.
4. What are the implications of the truth of this covenant to our relationship with the Lord and our salvation in Christ?
5. What does this covenant reveal about the nature and character of our God?

2 | The Covenant of Works

Setting the Scene

The opening pages of Scripture tell us that in the beginning God created the heavens and the earth (Gen. 1:1). Over a period of six days, he created the entire universe *ex nihilo* (out of nothing). The pinnacle of his work of creation was man. Genesis 1:27 tells us that, "God created man in his own image, in the image of God he created him; male and female he created them." God put the first man and woman, Adam and Eve, in a garden that he planted, the Garden of Eden, and blessed them with everything they needed, loving them as his own people. It was there that God made the first covenant between himself and man, the covenant of works.

What is the Covenant of Works?

The covenant of works is a conditional covenant that God made with Adam, as the first man and representative of the human race, in the Garden of Eden. It is for this reason that the covenant of works is sometimes called the Adamic covenant. God promised to bless and sustain Adam with life in the Garden. Yet God expected Adam to reciprocate in love to him, expressed through obedience. If he disobeyed him, God would curse him. Adam's works of obedience were the way in which he would obtain the reward from God: blessing and life. His obedience had to be perfect and ongoing. The Westminster Confession of Faith, 7.1-2, describes it in this manner:

> *The distance between God and the creature is so great, that although reasonable creatures do owe obedience unto him as their Creator, yet they could never have any fruition of him as their blessedness and reward, but by some voluntary condescension on God's part, which he hath been pleased to express by way of covenant. The first covenant made with man was a covenant of works, wherein life was promised to Adam; and in him to his posterity, upon condition of perfect and personal obedience.*

Though the text of Genesis 1-3 never calls God's arrangement with Adam a covenant, it is clear from the nature of the arrangement that it most certainly is a covenant. As we shall see below, it contains all the features of a covenant: an oath, stipulations, threats for breaking the covenant and blessings for keeping the covenant.[18] Later in the biblical narrative, in Hosea 6:7, the Bible explicitly calls this a covenant, "like Adam [Israel] transgressed the covenant."[19]

The Stipulations of the Covenant

Genesis 2:15-17 says:

> *The LORD God took the man and put him in the garden of Eden to work it and keep it. And the LORD God commanded the man, saying, "You may surely eat of every tree of the garden, but of the tree of the knowledge of good and evil you shall not eat, for in the day that you eat of it you shall surely die."*

Here we can see the stipulations of the covenant: Adam must work and keep the garden. He must further obey God's word to him. He can eat of any tree in the garden except for the tree of the knowledge of good and evil. If he were to do this, he would incur a covenant curse, death. In essence God promised: obey and live, disobey and die.

The Breaking of the Covenant and the Covenant Curse

In Genesis 3 we see that Adam and Eve were seduced by the words of the serpent and ate from the tree from which God had forbidden them to

---

[18] Kevin DeYoung, 'Afterword: Why Covenant Theology?' in *Covenant Theology: Biblical, Theological, and Historical Perspectives*, eds. Guy Prentiss Waters, J. Nicholas Reid, and John R. Muether (Wheaton: Crossway, 2020), 590.

[19] Some have questioned the use of this verse to justify the covenant of works, saying that Hosea is referring to a place named "Adam" where Israel broke a covenant, not Adam's breaking of the covenant in the Garden of Eden. In response to this objection, it can be said that there is no record in Scripture of Israel breaking a covenant at a place called Adam. Instead there are other examples in Scripture of references back to Adam, the man, in order to make a theological point, e.g. Job 31:33, Romans 5:12, 1 Corinthians 15:45. Also the preceding verse 6 of Hosea 6 speaks about God desiring steadfast love and not sacrifice, showing God's desire before the fall. This would favour the reference of "Adam" to refer to the man, and not the place.

eat. They disobeyed God and thereby broke the covenant, falling into sin. The result of this was that God confronted them and pronounced covenant curses upon them. In Genesis 3:16-19, we see that these are: pain in child birth for Eve and a desire to usurp her husband (3:16), and a cursed, hard existence of toil on earth and ultimate death for Adam (3:17-19). Both were then expelled from the Garden, which represented God's life, blessing, abundance and protection, to live on the harsh earth where they would experience a cursed existence, separated from God, and ultimately death.

The Nature of Life and Death

The "life" in question here is everlasting life. God promised Adam everlasting life if he obeyed his Word. This is why the sign of the covenant of works is the Tree of Life, as it pointed to eternal life. This covenant sign clearly showed Adam the reward for his obedience to the covenant. It was possible therefore for Adam to earn eternal life through his obedience to the terms of this covenant. God created Adam with the ability and power to obey his law. Perfect obedience to the covenant was therefore entirely possible for Adam, and he was not at all set up by God to fail. Yet because God created Adam with free will, it was possible for him to also disobey God. The penalty for Adam's disobedience was eternal death (Gen. 2:17). The extent of this death would be all encompassing: spiritual, physical and eternal death. Biblically-speaking, death is not just the end of physical existence, but also separation from God and all his goodness. After the fall, Adam and Eve did not physically die, but they immediately realised their spiritual death as they became aware of their nakedness (Gen. 3:7). They realised they had lost communion with God, that their relationship with him was impaired."[20]

Adam as the Representative of the Human Race

It is further important to note here that God made this covenant not exclusively with Adam, but with all his descendants. Every son of Adam and daughter of Eve is included in this covenant. Adam represented and acted on behalf of the entire human race. This means that the consequences

---

[20] Westminster Confession of Faith 4.2; Belgic Confession 14; Brown & Keele, Sacred Bond, 44-45..

of Adam's actions (breaking the covenant) were passed down to all his children. Sin, death and the curse have been inherited by every single human being because of Adam breaking this covenant. We can see the practical outworking of this truth throughout human history. Mankind's propensity is always to sin and rebel against God. Because of Adam's fall into sin, every human being in their natural state is totally depraved. This means that every part of our being is affected by sin. We are born dead in our sins and trespasses (Eph. 2:1), slaves to our sins (Rom. 6:17) and enemies of God (Rom. 5:10). We do not possess the free will to choose God, as in our depraved state, we are unable to even seek him (Rom. 3:11).[21]

In the Bible we see that Adam's descendants continued their depraved rebellion against God. Even their attempts to try their best to obey God always fell short. Israel's history shows this too. They try to please God, but are never able to perfectly obey him because of their sin. They end up in exile because of their continued rebellion against God.[22]

One or Two Covenants?

Not everyone has agreed with the idea that the covenant that God established between himself and Adam was a covenant of works. It has been argued by some that God showed grace to Adam before the fall by providing him with everything he could possibly need to live in the Garden. This was all granted to him before God required him to obey his law. It is for this reason that some theologians argue that God's covenant with Adam was a gracious covenant, an administration of the one covenant of grace that stretches across redemptive history. They therefore argue for a mono-covenantal framework as opposed to a bi-covenantal framework (two covenants: covenant of works and covenant of grace).[23]

There are important implications for the denial of the covenant of works, in favour of a mono-covenantal framework. As we shall soon see,

---

[21] Canons of Dort III & IV.2-3, Westminster Confession of Faith 6.

[22] Thomas Watson, *A Body of Divinity* (Edinburgh: Banner of Truth Trust, 1965), 129-130.

[23] Karl Barth is one of the most prominent theologians who has argued for a mono-covenantal framework. See, for example, Karl Barth, *Church Dogmatics, 14 vols.*, eds. G.W. Bromiley and T.F. Torrance (Edinburgh: T & T Clark, 1936-68), IV/1:62.

the covenant of works lays the foundation for the gospel. Why then is it necessary to view the covenant of works as law-based, conditional covenant, as classic Reformed theology has argued, and not as a gracious covenant? The reason is that there was no sin before the fall and therefore no need for grace in order to forgive sins. The grace which we find later in the covenant of grace is the grace of Christ: the undeserved gift of forgiveness of sins.[24]

Was not God's relationship with Adam before the fall gracious in nature? Did not God provide him with everything necessary in order to enjoy abundant life in the garden? This is certainly true, God's condescension to Adam to enter into a covenant with him and freely grant him abundant gifts and favour was indeed gracious. So in this sense there is grace in the covenant of works. Yet this grace should be distinguished from the saving grace that characterises the covenant of grace. John Fesko continues:

> *God voluntarily condescends to Adam and showers him with gifts in the creation, a sacramental manifestation of His love. God gave of Himself in love to Adam and looked for Adam to return this love to Him.*[25]

While God's actions with Adam before the fall were certainly gracious, we should rather describe God's covenantal arrangement with Adam as one of love, expressed through law-keeping. Because Adam was created good and in sinless perfection by God, he was able to love God by keeping the law and thus potentially fulfil the terms of the covenant. This is precisely why the Westminster Confession of Faith 4.2 says that Adam had the law of God written in his heart, and power to fulfil it. Had Adam obeyed, God would have granted him the gift of eternal life. Yet tragically he fell into sin, and it would be left up to the last Adam to fulfil the terms of this covenant, thus earning eternal life through his perfect obedience.[26]

---

[24] Richard P. Belcher, 'The Covenant of Works in the Old Testament' in *Covenant Theology: Biblical, Theological, and Historical Perspectives,* eds. Guy Prentiss Waters, J. Nicholas Reid, and John R. Muether (Wheaton: Crossway, 2020), 69.

[25] J.V. Fesko, *Adam and the Covenant of Works* (Fearn: Christian Focus Publications, 2021), 396.

[26] Fesko, *Adam and the Covenant of Works,* 416-417.

The covenant of works therefore must be firmly distinguished from the covenant of grace – they are not one in the same covenant. Through the covenant of works, God sets out the promise of eternal life upon condition of perfect obedience. Because of Adam's fall, mankind has been unable to obey this first covenant. That is why it pleased God to make a second covenant, the covenant of grace, where forgiveness of sins and eternal life are offered freely through faith in Christ.[27] Francis Turretin expresses it like this:

> *For in the former [covenant of works], God as Creator demands perfect obedience from innocent man with the promise of life and eternal happiness; but in the latter [covenant of grace], God as Father promises salvation in Christ to the fallen man under the condition of faith. The former rests upon the work of man; the latter upon the grace of God alone. The former upon a just Creator; the latter upon a merciful Redeemer. The former was made with innocent man without a mediator; the latter was made with fallen man by the intervention of a mediator.*[28]

The Works Principle

The principle that is clear in the covenant of works is that everlasting life must be earned.[29] This is what is called a "works principle". Everlasting life can only be gained by obeying God's Word, his law. Everlasting life is not given for free, there is a price for it and that price is perfect obedience. It can only be obtained by Someone who is perfectly righteous.

If the story ends there, it is really depressing as none of us is able to fulfil the terms of this covenant which require perfect obedience. In our depravity, we do not even seek after God, let alone do his will! Yet, thank God, there is Someone who has fulfilled the terms of this covenant.

---

[27] Westminster Confession of Faith 7.2-3; Herman Bavinck. *Reformed Dogmatics, vol. 2, God and Creation,* ed. John Bolt, trans. John Vriend. (Grand Rapids: Baker Academic, 2008), 564-571; Bavinck, Reformed Dogmatics, vol. 3, 224-228.

[28] Francis Turretin, *Institutes of Elenctic Theology,* ed. James T. Dennison, Jr., trans. George Musgrave Giger (Philadelphia: P&R Publishing, 1992), I:575.

[29] The Westminster Confession of Faith 7.2 states it like this: "The first covenant made with man was a covenant of works, wherein life was promised to Adam; and in him to his posterity, upon condition of perfect and personal obedience."

Jesus and the Covenant of Works

Turning to the New Testament, Romans 5:12-19 says:

> *Therefore, just as sin came into the world through one man, and death through sin, and so death spread to all men because all sinned—for sin indeed was in the world before the law was given, but sin is not counted where there is no law. Yet death reigned from Adam to Moses, even over those whose sinning was not like the transgression of Adam, who was a type of the one who was to come.*
>
> *But the free gift is not like the trespass. For if many died through one man's trespass, much more have the grace of God and the free gift by the grace of that one man Jesus Christ abounded for many. And the free gift is not like the result of that one man's sin. For the judgement following one trespass brought condemnation, but the free gift following many trespasses brought justification. For if, because of one man's trespass, death reigned through that one man, much more will those who receive the abundance of grace and the free gift of righteousness reign in life through the one man Jesus Christ.*
>
> *Therefore, as one trespass led to condemnation for all men, so one act of righteousness leads to justification and life for all men. For as by the one man's disobedience the many were made sinners, so by the one man's obedience the many will be made righteous.*

Further, 1 Corinthians 15:21-22 states: "For as by a man came death, by a man has come also the resurrection of the dead. For as in Adam all die, so also in Christ shall all be made alive."

From these texts we can see that: sin and death entered the world through Adam (by his breaking of the covenant of works). Grace, righteousness and life come to us through the last Adam, Jesus Christ. The disobedience of Adam led to all mankind being cursed. Yet the obedience of Jesus leads to the many being made righteous.[30]

---

[30] Guy Prentiss Waters, 'The Covenant of Works in the New Testament' in *Covenant Theology: Biblical, Theological, and Historical Perspectives*, eds. Guy Prentiss Waters, J. Nicholas Reid, and John R. Muether (Wheaton: Crossway, 2020), 85-90.

Jesus Christ is the Last Adam

Jesus Christ is the last Adam. He succeeded where the first Adam failed. Where Adam broke the covenant, Jesus upheld the covenant. Adam succumbed to temptation in the Garden, Jesus overcame temptation in the wilderness. The first Adam disobeyed, resulting in death, sin and curse for us. Yet the last Adam obeyed, resulting in life and blessing for those of us who believe in him. Jesus is the only truly Righteous One. Through his obedience, he has earned everlasting life. He then grants it to us as a gift of grace to be received by faith.

Because of the rebellion of the first Adam, God imputes to us his guilt and conveys to us our sinful nature.[31] The last Adam instead takes our sin upon himself on the cross enduring the covenant curse that our rebellion deserves (this is called Christ's passive obedience, as he endured suffering and punishment for sins) and he earns heaven by perfectly obeying the law during his time on earth (this is called Christ's active obedience, as he actively obeyed the law).

This means that our salvation is all a free gift of grace. It is not up to us to earn it, as Jesus already has. Therefore we are not saved by law keeping, as Jesus has already fulfilled the law. This is not to say that we become lawless. We will look at the significance of the law for the Christian in chapter 6. Instead we are saved by faith in Christ, through his obedience to the covenant of works.[32]

Conclusion

It should be clear here that the covenant of works is the foundation of the gospel. Christ paid our debt that none of us could ever afford. The terms of the covenant of works is that everlasting life is earned through perpetual obedience. Adam failed to earn it. So are we. But Christ, the only Righteous One, has earned it by his perfect obedience to the covenant, through his good works and taking upon himself the covenant curse. Trusting in him and his obedience to the covenant of works, he imputes his righteousness that he earned through his obedience, as a gracious gift

[31] Westminster Confession of Faith 6.3.

[32] Waters, 'The Covenant of Works in the New Testament' 85-90.

to us. Clothed in Christ's righteousness, as sinners, we are justified before our holy God, freed from the curse, forgiven of our sins and welcomed into his presence in heaven for all eternity.

Discussion Questions

1. What were the stipulations of the covenant that God made with Adam?
2. What were the consequences for Adam and Eve when they broke the covenant?
3. How is it that Adam is the representative of the entire human race? What are the implications of this for us?
4. Explain what is meant by the "works principle".
5. How does Jesus, as the last Adam, fulfil the covenant of works?
6. Explain why the covenant of works is the foundation of the gospel, and the basis of our justification in Christ.

3 | The Covenant of Grace

Setting the Scene

In Genesis 3, Adam and Eve obeyed the word of the serpent, rather than the Word of God, and committed the first sin. They broke the covenant of works that God had made with them, and they must face the penalty for their sin. The penalty for breaking the covenant, which God had promised in Genesis 2:17, was that they would "surely die."

The effects of their sin are immediate. The perfect relationship that Adam and Eve had is broken. They are now ashamed in each other's presence and so cover up their nakedness (Gen. 3:7). The perfect relationship that they enjoyed with the Lord is also broken, as they hide from God when he comes looking for them in the Garden (Gen. 3:8) and God expels them from the Garden, from his presence (Gen. 3:24). Because of this rupture in their relationship with God, they are now spiritually dead to God. Their default setting will not be to seek him and please him. Instead they, and mankind after them, are now "dead in trespasses and sins" (Eph. 2:1), and unable to even seek God (Rom. 3:11).

It seems that all is now lost. Having broken the covenant of works through their disobedience, Adam, and mankind after him, have been plunged into sin, separated from God and considered dead to him. They experience the covenant curse of death that God promised them.

Yet all is not lost. God has not given up on his people. As God delivers the covenant curses to the serpent, Eve and Adam in Genesis 3:14-19, God makes a promise in verse 15, that he will sovereignly save his people from the curse of sin and death. As Scripture unfolds, we see this promise as another covenant, the covenant of grace.

What is the Covenant of Grace?

The Westminster Confession of Faith 7.3 describes the covenant of grace in this way:

Man, by his fall, having made himself incapable of life by that covenant, the Lord was pleased to make a second, commonly called the covenant of grace; wherein he freely offereth unto sinners life and salvation by Jesus Christ; requiring of them faith in him, that they may be saved, and promising to give them unto all those that are ordained unto eternal life his Holy Spirit, to make them willing, and able to believe.

The covenant of grace is the one covenant through which all believers, all of God's chosen people, are saved. The covenant, though established in eternity in the form of the covenant of redemption, begins in time in Genesis 3:15 with God's promise to send a Saviour to crush the head of the serpent. It thus stretches across redemptive history, culminating in the coming of Christ.[33]

Because of its overarching nature, we find that it is administered in different ways during the course of redemptive history. For example, it is the same covenant of grace that is administered in the other covenants that God made with Adam (Gen. 3:15), Noah (Gen. 6-8), Abraham (Gen. 15, 17), Moses (Ex. 19-24), David (2 Sam. 7), and is eventually fulfilled in Christ in the New Covenant.[34]

---

[33] Brown & Keele, *Sacred Bond*, 58-59.

[34] The Westminster Confession of Faith, chapter 7.4-6, explains in more detail: "[4]This covenant of grace is frequently set forth in Scripture by the name of a testament, in reference to the death of Jesus Christ the Testator, and to the everlasting inheritance, with all things belonging to it, therein bequeathed. [5]This covenant was differently administered in the time of the law, and in the time of the gospel: under the law, it was administered by promises, prophecies, sacrifices, circumcision, the paschal lamb, and other types and ordinances delivered to the people of the Jews, all foresignifying Christ to come; which were, for that time, sufficient and efficacious, through the operation of the Spirit, to instruct and build up the elect in faith in the promised Messiah, by whom they had full remission of sins, and eternal salvation; and is called the old testament. [6]Under the gospel, when Christ, the substance, was exhibited, the ordinances in which this covenant is dispensed are the preaching of the Word, and the administration of the sacraments of baptism and the Lord's Supper: which, though fewer in number, and administered with more simplicity, and less outward glory, yet, in them, it is held forth in more fullness, evidence and spiritual efficacy, to all nations, both Jews and Gentiles; and is called the new testament. There are not therefore two covenants of grace, differing in substance, but one and the same, under various dispensations."
Richard P. Belcher, *The Fulfillment of the Promises of God: An explanation of Covenant Theology* (Fearn: Christian Focus Publications, 2020), 43.

While it has been administered in various ways, the substance of the covenant remains the same. In both the Old and New Testaments, the way in which God saves sinners is always the same: by grace alone, through faith alone and because of Christ alone. Jesus Christ is the one Mediator of the covenant of grace that unifies the one people of God throughout all time.

The covenant of grace is the outworking of the covenant of redemption. We saw in chapter 1 that this was the covenant where the Trinity covenanted in eternity to save God's people. This salvation was fulfilled in time through Jesus coming to earth, his perfect obedience to the point of death on the cross for the sins of his people. It was for Jesus a covenant of works (he earned heaven on our behalf), which was examined in the previous chapter. His obedience under the covenant of works is the foundation for the covenant of grace. The covenant of grace therefore applies to sinners the benefits that Christ earned through his fulfilment of the covenant of redemption: chiefly, the forgiveness of our sins and the promise of eternal life. Because Jesus has done this work on our behalf, we receive the promises of the covenant of grace as a gift.

The promise of the covenant of grace from God is that, "I will be your God, and you will be my people" (Ex. 6:7, Lev. 26:11-12, Jer. 31:33, Ezek. 37:26-27, Rev. 21:2-3). This is God's unbreakable promise to us through this covenant, that no matter what, he will always be our God and we will always be his people. This promise is not determined by our works or level of faith, nor jeopardised by our sin or doubts; but is instead guaranteed to us by the finished work of Jesus Christ. God has done all the work in this covenant. In this sense, the covenant of grace is unilateral – it is established and initiated entirely by God. Yet this does not mean that there are no obligations from our side in this covenant. While the covenant of grace is unilaterally established by God, a response is required from us. What is that response? Faith and repentance, both of which are only possible by the work of the Holy Spirit in our lives.[35] Without these, no one can

[35] The Westminster Larger Catechism explains in more detail in Q & A 32: "Q. *How is the grace of God manifested in the second covenant?* A. The grace of God is manifested in the second covenant, in that he freely provideth and offereth to sinners a mediator, and life and salvation by him; and requiring faith as the condition to interest them in him, promiseth and giveth his Holy Spirit to all his elect, to work in them that faith, with all other saving graces; and to enable them unto all holy obedience, as the evidence of the truth of their faith and thankfulness to God, and as the way which he hath appointed them to salvation."

be saved. This is why the Scripture declares in numerous places, "Believe in the Lord Jesus Christ, and you will be saved" (Acts 16:31, Rom. 10:6-13, Gal. 2:16).[36]

The Puritan, Thomas Watson (c. 1620-1686) writes concerning the nature of our obligation in the covenant of grace:

> *But are not works required in the covenant of grace? Yes. 'This is a faithful saying, that they which believe in God, be careful to maintain good works.' Titus 3:8. But the covenant of grace does not require works in the same manner as the covenant of works did. In the first covenant [covenant of works], works were required as the condition of life; in the second [covenant of grace], they are required only as the signs of life. In the first covenant, works were required as grounds of salvation; in the new covenant, they are required as evidences of our love to God. In the first, they were required to the justification of our persons; in the new, to the manifestation of our grace.*[37]

So God sovereignly secures our reception of the blessings of the covenant of grace in two ways. First, Christ keeps the covenant commands and endures the covenant curse for us. Second, the Holy Spirit invincibly applies transforming grace in us, giving us faith and repentance, as evidences of our love to God.

Biblical Evidence for the Covenant of Grace

The Protoevangelium – Genesis 3:15-24

After Adam and Eve sinned by disobeying God's Word and breaking the covenant of works that God had made with them, God grants them grace in the face of their rebellion. This is why this verse is often called the *protoevangelium* (first gospel), as it is the first time in Scripture that the gospel is preached:

---

[36] Derek W.H. Thomas, 'Covenant, Assurance, and the Sacraments' in *Covenant Theology: Biblical, Theological, and Historical Perspectives*, eds. Guy Prentiss Waters, J. Nicholas Reid, and John R. Muether (Wheaton: Crossway, 2020), 580-581; Watson, *A Body of Divinity*, 156.

[37] Watson, *A Body of Divinity*, 155-156.

> *I will put enmity between you [Satan] and the woman [Eve], and between your offspring [unbelievers] and her offspring [God's people]; he [the Messiah] shall crush your head, and you [Satan] shall bruise his heel. (3:15)*

> *And the Lord God made for Adam and for his wife garments of skins and clothed them... (3:21)*

How is it that the gospel is preached here? There are four parts to this gospel promise:

God puts enmity between Satan and Eve: He breaks the unholy covenant between them, which had been made at the Fall. God does not allow this sinful relationship to continue, so from this point on, the relationship is broken.

God puts enmity between Satan's offspring and Eve's offspring: God promises to preserve a people for himself, that are set apart from the offspring of the devil. From Genesis 4, we see a division in mankind, between the seed of the serpent and the seed of the woman. Adam's eldest son, Cain, turns out to be the seed of the serpent, as he murders his brother, Abel. Wickedness continues through his descendants, who are reprobate and enemies of God.

The line of the seed of the woman continues through Adam's youngest son, Seth, the godly lineage. God promises to one-day rescue them. These are the children of God's promise, the elect. They are all of God's people from all time, all of those who have believed in the promise. It is here that the church was formed!

God promises a Messiah who would one day crush Satan's head: The Hebrew word, *šûph*, can be translated as "bruise" which is often used in the English translations. Yet it can also be translated as "crush". God's promise here is that he will send a Champion, a Messiah, a male descendant of Eve, who will crush Satan's head. We see various forerunners of this Messiah in the Old Testament (for example, Noah, Abraham, Moses, Joseph, Joshua, Gideon and David) who all in some way point to him. Ultimately Jesus is the promised Messiah, the seed of Eve, who defeats Satan by dying on the cross, breaking the curse of sin and death. Initially, he would appear to have been bruised by Satan, as he died on the cross. Yet it was by his death that

Christ destroyed "the one who has the power of death, that is, the devil" (Heb. 2:14). Then, to demonstrate his victory, he rose again on the third day!

God clothes Adam and Eve in skins, pointing to the promise of Christ's righteousness: After the Fall, Adam and Eve become conscious of their sinfulness before God by covering their nakedness. God would have been just then and there to put both of them to death, as the penalty for sin is death. Yet, he shows them grace and instead of killing them, kills an animal, shedding its blood on their behalf. He then clothes them in its skin, hiding their guilt and shame. This points towards the sacrifice Christ will make on the cross, where his blood will be shed for our sins, and we will then be clothed in his righteousness, hiding our guilt and shame.[38]

Implications of the Covenant of Grace

We relate to God through Grace, not Law

We do not earn God's favour by law keeping, nor by our level of faith, or spiritual techniques or how much we tithe. Nor can we fall out of God's favour and love by our sins, our doubts or our backsliding. To be sure, habitual sin will always be destructive in our lives and God may discipline us as his children. Yet we can never lose our salvation because of it.[39] At the same time, true faith in Christ will always lead to good works and obedience. These are an outflow of having received God's grace. We do not earn it through our good works. Instead we relate to God purely through what Christ has already done for us. This means that we can approach God boldly and with confidence as his sons, as Jesus has shed his blood for our sins (Heb. 10:19-25).

We can have absolute assurance of our everlasting salvation in Christ through the covenant of grace. Because God has covenanted to always be our God and we his people, because of his work in Christ, we can know with certainty that our salvation is secure in him. His steadfast love to us, his people is sure. Our sins have been removed from us as far as the east is from the west (Ps. 103:12). His Spirit has caused us to be born again of imperishable seed (1 Pet. 1:23). In Christ, his promise is that he is always faithful to us, even when we are faithless (2 Tim. 2:13). He promises to

---

[38] Brown & Keele, *Sacred Bond*, 60-65.

[39] Westminster Confession of Faith 11.5.

faithfully preserve us in his grace until the end (Phil. 1:6).[40] Indeed, nothing in heaven and earth can separate us from the love of God in Christ Jesus our Lord! (Rom. 8:38-39). Our obvious response to this gift of grace is to live with grateful hearts, overflowing obedience to his Word, for his glory. But our level of obedience does not secure our salvation – only the perfect obedience of Christ does!

This truth shows up the problems of Roman Catholic and Arminian doctrine in this regard which teach that we are saved by grace, but stay in by works. In these systems it is possible to fall away from God and lose our salvation if we sin grievously, or fail to perform enough good works. The result of this type of teaching is that we remain insecure in our salvation, never quite knowing if we are good enough for God. It is a de facto salvation by works system, which is really no gospel at all. Thank God that we are instead saved in this unbreakable covenant of grace through Christ, who grants us our salvation *by grace*, as a gift!

The Bible is One Book with One Story

The overarching nature of the covenant of grace also shows us that all Scripture is telling us essentially one story, and leading to a single end point. From Genesis to Revelation, the Bible points to Christ and reveals his gospel of grace. This is why Jesus says in Luke 24:44-47:

> *"Everything written about me in the Law of Moses and the Prophets and the Psalms must be fulfilled." Then he opened their minds to understand the Scriptures, and said to them, "Thus it is written, that the Christ should suffer and on the third day rise from the dead, and that repentance and forgiveness of sins should be proclaimed in his name to all nations, beginning from Jerusalem.*

Jesus says here that the entire Old Testament (Law, Prophets and Psalms) is all about him. Even the central tenants of the gospel: his death and resurrection on the cross and forgiveness of sins, the heart of the covenant of grace, is the underlying theme of all the Scriptures. Therefore, the point of Scripture is not to lead us to moralism: that we should be brave like David, or be wise like Solomon. Nor are we to read the various stories in the Bible in isolation, as we would some bed-time tales. Instead we are to

---

[40] Canons of Dort V.3.

read the Bible as one, unified story about Christ and his gospel: the seed of the woman who will crush the serpent, forgive our sins, and redeem for himself a people of the covenant. The many stories contained in Scripture only make real sense when we read them as a part of God's one bigger story, which is to save a people for himself through Christ.[41]

Conclusion

Thankfully, all is not lost in Adam's fall into sin. God makes another covenant, a covenant of grace, where he promises to save his people by his grace, forgiving our sins. It is in Genesis 3:15 that we first see evidence of this covenant. We see here that we have not only a prophecy about the coming Messiah, but the magnificent promise from God, this covenant of grace, the gospel, that he will be our God, and we his people. This promise unfolds in the pages of the rest of Scripture, culminating in Jesus Christ.

Discussion Questions

1. Explain the central promise of the covenant of grace.
2. Explain how the gospel is preached in Genesis 3:15.
3. How does the truth of the covenant of grace affect how we relate to God?
4. Though we have been saved by grace in Christ, what is our appropriate response? What are our covenantal obligations in the covenant of grace?
5. How does the covenant of grace affect how we read and understand the Scriptures?
6. In what way does the covenant of grace give us assurance of our salvation through Christ?

---

[41] Three excellent books that show how all Scripture points to Christ are: Dennis Johnson, *Him We Proclaim, Preaching Christ from All the Scriptures* (Phillipsburg: P&R Publishing, 2007), *Walking with Jesus through His Word: Discovering Christ in All the Scriptures* (Phillipsburg, P&R Publishing, 2015) and Edmund P. Clowney, *The Unfolding Mystery: Discovering Christ in the Old Testament* (Leicester: Inter-Varsity Press, 1988).

4 | The Noahic Covenant

Setting the Scene

The result of Adam's fall into sin plunges all mankind after him into a continual downward spiral of sin and depravity. His own son, Cain, murders his brother, Abel in cold blood (Gen. 4:8). Most of Adam's descendants continue down this path of sin and rebellion against God. In Genesis 6, God is dismayed at the great wickedness of man, "that every intention of the thoughts of his heart was only evil continually" (Gen. 6:5). As a result of man's wickedness, God resolves to destroy mankind on the earth. As the penalty for sin is death, God sends a great flood across the face of the earth that will drown all humans, as punishment for their sin. Yet, out of all of mankind, God chooses Noah, a descendant of Eve, in the line of Seth, and his family. God makes a covenant with Noah in Genesis 6:18 through which he and his family will be saved by God from the flood. They are saved from the flood, as God instructs Noah to build a great ark on which they, and two of every animal, will live for the duration of the flood. Once the flood has subsided, God makes a second covenant with Noah, which will be examined in this chapter (Gen. 8:20-9:17).[42]

What is the Noahic Covenant?

In this covenant, God promised Noah that he would never again destroy the earth and that he would sustain all mankind after him with food from the earth. Another name for this covenant is the common grace covenant. The reason for this is to distinguish between grace that is common and grace that is special. What then is common grace? It is God's undeserved kindness to all people, regardless whether they are believers or unbelievers. It describes the common blessings that God has showered upon the entire human race, whether it be sunshine, rain, food, possessions, wisdom,

---

[42] Miles V. Van Pelt, 'The Noahic Covenant of the Covenant of Grace' in *Covenant Theology: Biblical, Theological, and Historical Perspectives*, eds. Guy Prentiss Waters, J. Nicholas Reid, and John R. Muether (Wheaton: Crossway, 2020), 118.

culture, music or art. It also describes God's restraining hand over human sinfulness. The fact that depraved humanity is still capable of much good is only due to God's common grace.[43]

This is in contrast to God's special grace. God's special grace is the grace that he grants only to his chosen people, the church. This is what was examined in the previous chapter, under the covenant of grace. God's special grace is his saving grace through Jesus Christ to forgive the sins of his people, restore them in relationship with the Father and seal them for redemption in Christ by his Spirit. These blessings are not common, in that they are not granted to every single human being (that would be the heresy of universalism, the belief that everyone is saved). Yet the blessings of God's common grace are common to both God's people and unbelievers, all of mankind. The Noahic covenant is therefore God's gracious promise to all of creation, that he will never again destroy the earth, and that he will sustain it until the return of Christ.[44]

What does the Bible Teach?

God's common grace covenant with Noah is taught in Genesis 8:20-9:17.

The Nature of God's Promises

We can see here the nature of the promise of this covenant. In Genesis 8:20, Noah makes a burnt offering of some of the animals and birds to the Lord as an act of thanksgiving for delivering him through the flood. The Lord then smells the aroma of the offering and makes Noah two promises. The first promise is that he will never again destroy the earth by flooding it, because of the wickedness of man (8:21). The second promise is that God promises to sustain the earth through the normal cycle of seasons (8:22). God will ensure that the climate of the earth will provide the right conditions for crops to grow and animals to flourish.

God makes these promises to Noah and mankind after him, despite the utter depravity of the human race. The state of man is no better after the

---

[43] David VanDrunen, *Living in God's Two Kingdoms: A Biblical Vision for Christianity and Culture* (Wheaton: Crossway, 2010), 78-81.

[44] VanDrunen, *Living in God's Two Kingdoms*, 81; Brown & Keele, *Sacred Bond*, 74-75.

flood than before. God grants the human race life under the sun even though they still deserve punishment. This promise is not dependent on man's behaviour, but simply an unconditional promise from God to sustain him regardless.

The Parties of the Covenant

It is clear here that God is the one making the covenant. He initiates it. Yet he makes it, not just with one other party, but with multiple parties. He makes it with Noah and his sons (9:1), but also with their descendants (9:9) and the animals (the livestock, birds and every beast, 9:10). Noah functions as the representative of all future humanity. It is clear here too that the covenant is made with all of mankind without exception – hence it is common – for all. It is non-redemptive in nature, there is no promise to save people from sins, but instead to preserve the natural order in the world so that life can continue to exist.

The Sign of the Covenant

The sign of the Noahic covenant is the rainbow (9:12-17). God explicitly calls it the sign of the covenant in the text. The rainbow serves as a reminder to God and us that God will never again destroy the earth. What then is the significance of the rainbow in particular? The Hebrew word used for rainbow (*qešet*) can also mean "bow". In Ancient Near East culture, their gods were portrayed with bows stretched out in front of them as they went into war. After the battle, the bow was then hung upwards, symbolising peace after the war. The rainbow then, symbolises God's own bow being hung upwards in the sky, signifying peace, that he will not destroy the earth again. It is an incredible sign that serves to remind us to this day of God's faithfulness in this covenant every time we see it in the sky.[45]

A Gracious Covenant

As this covenant has been made unilaterally by God, all the terms of the covenant are made by him and kept by him. It is therefore a gracious covenant. God has promised never again to destroy the world and he has promised to sustain all of mankind until Jesus returns. Those promises are not dependent on us, or how sinful mankind becomes. It is despite

---

[45] Brown & Keele, *Sacred Bond*, 76-78.

our sinfulness and rebellion that God upholds these incredible promises. Despite wars, injustice, terror and various forms of evil, God will still send rain and sunshine to us.

Covenantal Regulations

While the covenant is unilateral and unconditional in the sense that God has promised to fulfil and uphold all his promises to us, despite our sinfulness, God does make some regulations in the process of making the covenant. These regulations are not covenant conditions, the covenant is not dependent on us keeping these things. What then are these regulations?

Marriage and Procreation: In Genesis 9:1, God says to Noah and his sons that they must be fruitful and multiply. He says the same to the animals earlier in 8:17 – both humans and animals must procreate and fill the earth. Marriage is assumed in this regulation, therefore marriage and procreation are a good and normal part of society.

Lordship over Animals and Plants: God also gives to Noah all things for food (9:3). Noah can eat all animals and plants. God has given mankind lordship over the animals. God gave us food to enjoy, therefore God's provision of food is more than just sustenance, but should cause us to give thanks to God as our Provider.

The Goodness of Labour: The implication of this is that work is good. If we are to eat livestock and crops as a gift from God, that means that the cultivation of them is a good thing. God sees labour as a positive thing, and desires that we should all work for his glory.

The Institution of the State: The next regulation that we see here is in verse 6, where God says that whoever sheds the blood of man, by man shall his blood be shed, as man is made in God's image. This not only shows that murder is wrong, but also that man has the right and duty to punish murderers with the death penalty. The reason for this is that we are created in God's image, so killing a fellow human is tantamount to an assault on God himself.

What we see here is the foundation of the institution of the state by God. One of the main roles of governments is to protect human life by administering justice (Rom. 13:3-4).[46] Though there is no perfect government, God has delegated power and authority to them in order to administer justice so that human depravity is restrained. This is why the New Testament affirms the God-ordained role of the state in wielding the sword. Christians are to submit to their earthly rulers, as God has placed them there (Rom. 13:1). Their authority is however always subject to God, and should Christians ever be placed in a situation where their obedience to God and his Word is compromised by state compulsion, we should have the attitude of the apostles in Acts 5:29, who declared, "We must obey God rather than men."[47]

Natural Law: What this also tells us is that as a part of God's common grace to mankind, he has given every human an innate sense of right and wrong. His law is written on all hearts, even those who try to suppress it. Even though human inclination is bent on evil and rebellion, God's natural law is imprinted on our consciences and written on our hearts (Rom. 2:14-15).[48] This means that as there is a general awareness of natural law among sinful man, we do not act as badly as we could.[49]

The Coming Seed of the Woman

The Noahic covenant anticipates the coming of the promised Messiah, Jesus Christ. God promised Adam and Eve in Genesis 3:15 that he would send the offspring of the woman who would come to crush the head of the serpent in the fullness of time. Common grace enables this promise to unfold. God's restraining hand over the world has allowed for Jesus to be born of a woman, die on the cross and rise again on the third day, defeating sin, death and the curse. Even after Jesus ascended to heaven, God did not bring his promised final judgement. Common grace is the reason why this is still being delayed and humans can live in this age and enjoy the many blessings from God and have the opportunity to hear the gospel of grace in Christ preached to them. There will be a Day, however, when common grace will come to an end. On that Day, Jesus will return and set

---

[46] Belgic Confession 36.

[47] David VanDrunen, *Politics after Christendom: Political Theology in a fractured world* (Grand Rapids: Zondervan, 2020), 104-113.

[48] Westminster Confession of Faith 4.2.

[49] VanDrunen, *Politics after Christendom*, 124-125.

all injustices right – unbelievers and evildoers will be punished, they will face God's wrath for their sin, while those in Christ will be raised to life with him and enjoy life in the new creation in his presence for all eternity.

Implications of Common Grace

God gives sinners a second chance

When Adam and Eve sinned in Eden, God was within his right to execute them on the spot as he had promised them in the covenant of works that if they were to disobey him, they would surely die (Gen. 2:17). He did not. Instead he clothed them in skins, and allowed them to continue to live on earth, enjoying his gracious provision – this was his common grace to them. In the same way he treats mankind. He does not destroy all sinners now, as he would be in his right to do, as sin deserves the penalty of death. Instead, he gives all humans a chance to live on this earth, enjoy his many blessings in this life and have the opportunity to repent and receive Christ.

God restrains sin

It is only because of common grace that the world is not as bad as it could be. Because mankind is totally depraved, incapable of doing good on its own because of original sin, the world should be a totally horrific place. While there is certainly evil and injustice present in the world, caused by man's sinfulness, it is not nearly as bad as it could be. We see that even unbelievers are capable of doing good things – building civilisation, being compassionate, loving others, developing culture, doing and making beautiful things. These things are only possible because of common grace – God's restraining hand over mankind's sinful hearts.

The Preservation of some sense of Truth and Morality

As we have seen earlier, the existence of common grace preserves in mankind a basic sense of right and wrong, of morality. As God writes his law on our hearts, as much as we can rebel against it, deep down we all know that we are doing wrong. Of course God does harden sinners' hearts who are persistent in evil and gives them over to their lusts. But overall most people understand that murder, adultery and theft are wrong. They only come to this conclusion because of natural law, the law that God writes on every heart. This basic sense of morality, which comes from natural law, forms the basis for most legal codes in the world.

Engagement with the Secular Realm

Common grace allows us to have a healthy view of culture and the state. Historically there have been two broad views concerning this issue. The first view has been that of the Roman Catholic Church, which especially during the medieval period, sought to dominate the secular realm. An obvious example is the way in which the Roman Empire was Christianized after 313 AD under the Emperor Constantine. This was the advent of what became known as Christendom. The Pope was the spiritual ruler over most of Europe for over a thousand years. In addition to ecclesial authority, the papacy exerted immense political influence across Europe too. This meant that the church's authority was not limited to spiritual affairs, but extended into the political sphere as well.

While this is no longer the case today in Europe, some in the church still aspire to do this with statements such as, "take over the culture", "redeem the culture" or "take back our government for Christ". While we should always preach Christ and his gospel in our community and nation, we should not desire to return to the era of Christendom. That usually never ends well for the church, as it often results in the abuse of political and ecclesial power. There are unfortunately too many examples of this in history, as the Crusades, Inquisitions and the various wars of religion, all took place when the church had a great influence in political power in Europe.

At the other end of the spectrum, there has been the tendency to retreat from culture, seeing it as pervasively and intrinsically evil. Historically the Anabaptist movement (birthed in the radical Reformation of the 1500s) has adopted this position. Anabaptist communities (their modernday descendants are the Mennonites, Amish and Brethren communities) completely separated themselves from society, seeing it as unholy. They rebelled against governments, retreated from cultural things, they saw all secular art, music, dancing, playing cards, and any kind of worldly pleasures (like alcohol and smoking) as intrinsically evil.

There are still tendencies in the church to go in this direction. We find forms of legalism and asceticism expressed in the view that drinking alcohol is in itself sinful. Similarly, activities such as dancing, watching secular movies, listening to secular music, wearing nice clothes, or the enjoyment of any simple God-given pleasures on this earth are frowned upon.

A good understanding of common grace helps us engage healthily with the secular world and culture. Because of God's goodness in creation, the secular state and culture should not be viewed as always negative. We should be free to engage in the world, exercising Christian liberty, and enjoying the many blessings that God has given us through it, whether it be through the arts, music, good food and wine, or going to a concert. We should also recognise that God has instituted state institutions which are there to guide us and lead us. The church should therefore have no desire to take them over. A clear distinction between church and state is entirely biblical. Jesus says in John 18:36, "My kingdom is not of this world." The role of the church is not to entangle itself with political power. Rather it must faithfully preach the gospel, worship the Lord, administer the sacraments and disciple believers. This is why the Westminster Confession of Faith 31.4 says that the church is to "handle, or conclude nothing but that which is ecclesiastical" and is "not to intermeddle with civil affairs which concern the commonwealth." The role of the state is to run the government, maintain justice and defend the defenceless. The state is to ensure religious liberty for all, but must not interfere in the affairs of the church. The Westminster Confession of Faith 23.3 says in this regard, "Civil magistrates may not assume to themselves the administration of the Word and sacraments; or the power of the keys of the kingdom of heaven; or, in the least, interfere in matters of faith."

We should never forget though, that the system of the world is corrupted by sin and is following the spirit of this age. God has promised that he will judge the nations on the Last Day. Hence we should not seek to become one with the world and blend in so much that we are indistinguishable from unbelievers. We should unashamedly proclaim the gospel in this present age.

The Enjoyment of God's Blessings

Common grace gives us the freedom to enjoy the many natural blessings that God has granted to all mankind. Psalm 104:14-15 says, "You cause the grass to grow for the livestock and plants for man to cultivate, that he may bring forth food from the earth and wine to gladden the heart of man, oil to make his face shine and bread to strengthen man's heart." God has blessed us with wine, oil and bread so that we can enjoy these small pleasures of life and in turn give him thanks.

God gives gifts to all people on earth, both believers and unbelievers. He has enabled people to pursue good things such as the arts, science and music. He has gifted people with the desire to grow and develop human civilisation – to invent things, to create, to work, to build, to farm and harness the land. Psalm 145:9, 16 says, "The LORD is good to all, and his mercy is over all that he has made... You open your hand; you satisfy the desire of every living thing." God shows his love and reveals his common grace to all people. Matthew 5:45 says, "he makes the sun rise on the evil and on the good, and sends rain on the just and on the unjust."

Conclusion

Ultimately the Noahic covenant gives us great assurance that nothing can thwart God's plan. Whatever calamities we may face this side of eternity – war, famine, pandemics, political instability, natural disasters, all kinds of evil – we know that God still remembers his covenant with us when the rainbow shines. He has promised that he will not destroy the earth and that he will preserve all of creation by his grace. Even when the Lord permits great trials and tragedies in our lives, we can know that they will not be as bad as they could be, because God is sovereign and has his hand over us in the midst of these times.

Yet, this is only a temporary reprieve. While judgement has been delayed in the Noahic covenant, it will surely come when Jesus Christ returns. Second Corinthians 5:10 says, "For we must all appear before the judgement seat of Christ, so that each one may receive what is due for what he has done in the body, whether good or evil." Only if found in Christ, who alone forgives sins, will we be delivered from this judgement and welcomed as God's own sons for everlasting life with him in the new creation.

Discussion Questions

1. How do we distinguish between common and special grace?
2. What is the central promise of the Noahic covenant?
3. Explain what natural law is, and how God uses it to restrain evil in the world.
4. How does our understanding of common grace affect how Christians should relate to the culture around us?
5. What are the respective roles of the church and state? Why is it important that we maintain a distinction between the two?
6. How does common grace give Christians freedom to enjoy good things in this life?

5 | The Abrahamic Covenant

Setting the Scene

In the previous chapter, we saw that God judged the depravity of man by flooding the earth. After the flood, Noah and his family started a new humanity. Yet the problem of sin remained. His descendants continued to rebel against God, culminating in the building of the Tower of Babel (Gen. 11:1-9). This act was a testimony to human wickedness, a rejection of God and a monument to man's selfishness.

Because of mankind's increasing fall into sin, God called a man called Abram and made a covenant with him. Abram was born after Noah, through the line of his son Shem. He was son of Terah, from Ur in the land of the Chaldeans.

God's Covenant with Abraham

In Genesis 12, God spoke to Abram and promised him that he will make of him a great nation, that he will bless him and make his name great (12:2). He also promised to give to his offspring the land of Canaan. In Genesis 15, God returned to Abram in a vision and made a covenant with him. Despite the fact that Abram and his barren wife Sarai were nearly a hundred years old and without children of their own, he promised him that his offspring will be as numerous as the stars of the heavens (15:5). Abram "believed the Lord, and he counted it to him as righteousness" (15:6). Abram was justified by faith alone.

This clearly shows us that this is a gracious covenant, an administration of the one covenant of grace, stretching across redemptive history. God made this covenant with Abram, not dependent on any of his works, but entirely dependent on God's promises to him. Abram just believed it, and righteousness was counted to him as a gift (Rom. 4:1-6). As a part of this covenant God reaffirmed his promise to give the land of Canaan to his descendants (12:7).

God then commanded Abram to get a heifer, a goat, a ram, a dove and a pigeon. He commanded him to cut each animal (except the birds) in half, and then Abram fell into a deep sleep. Verse 17 then tells us that a smoking fire pot and flaming torch passed between the pieces.

What is the significance of this? This was how covenants were made in the Ancient Near East between two parties. Animals were cut in half and both parties would have to walk between the slaughtered animals.[50] The dead animals served as a vivid picture of what would happen to either party if they were to break the covenant – they would end up like those slaughtered animals! This clearly displayed the penalty for breaking the covenant, which was a cursed death. In fact in the Hebrew Bible, the idiom used for "to make a covenant" is literally "to cut a covenant" (*kârăt bərît*) because cutting up animals was the way covenants were sealed.

What is unusual in Genesis 15 however, is that both parties of the covenant do not walk through the slaughtered animals. Only one does, as Abram was sleeping. We saw that in verse 17 a smoking fire pot and flaming torch passed between the pieces. These both symbolise God's presence.[51] The point is here that it is only God who passed through the animals and not Abram.

Why is this important? The nature of the Abrahamic covenant is that it is unilateral. God promised to do everything. Abram did not have to do anything to earn God's covenant blessings. His only obligation was to receive the covenant promises by faith. This is why the Abrahamic covenant is an administration of the covenant of grace. Further, it is God alone who promised to take upon himself the covenant penalty. He promised to end up like the slaughtered animals, to carry the curse, if the covenant were to be broken.

In Genesis 17, God reaffirmed his covenant with Abram. He promised Abram that his offspring would be multiplied (17:2) and that he would be the father of a multitude of nations (17:4). God changed his name to Abraham, meaning "father of a multitude" (ab = father in Hebrew) (17:5),

---

[50] See for example Jeremiah 34:18-20.

[51] See for example Exodus 13:21-22 where God's presence with Israel was in a pillar of fire.

and Sarai's name to Sarah, meaning "princess" (17:15). God promised to make Abraham into many nations, kings shall come from him, and this covenant will be established as an everlasting covenant through all their generations (17:6,8). Again he promised Abraham's offspring the land of Canaan as an "everlasting possession" (17:8). In response, God required Abraham to "walk before me, and be blameless" (17:1). He also instructed Abraham to circumcise every male in the covenant community as a sign of the covenant (17:11). From that point on, every male child at eight days old was to receive the sign of the covenant (17:12). Those males who were not circumcised were to be cut off from God's people (17:10-14). Lastly God promised Abraham a son of promise. Sarah, who was barren, will miraculously bear a son called Isaac, through whom the covenant will continue and from whose seed the Messiah will come (17:19).[52]

Though the Abrahamic covenant is clearly a gracious covenant, Genesis 17 shows that God expected a response from Abraham. Abraham had covenant obligations to fulfil. He could not earn any of the covenant promises from God: the land, the promise of blessing and a nation – these were all to be received as a gift of grace from God. Yet God required that Abraham and his descendants must respond in faith to his promises in obedience. They must walk uprightly, in obedience to God, and they must be circumcised in order to enjoy the blessings and benefits of the covenant.[53]

How was this Covenant Fulfilled?

God's covenant with Abraham is fulfilled in two stages:

First Stage

It is fulfilled in the history of Israel. God kept his promise to Abraham and Sarah to provide them with an heir. While they had sinfully tried to make their own plan with Hagar, who bore Ishmael, God was faithful and Sarah conceived and bore Isaac, the son of promise. Later, Isaac's son,

[52] Meredith G. Kline, *Kingdom Prologue: Genesis foundations for a covenantal worldview* (Eugene: Wipf & Stock Publishers, 2006), 296-299; John Scott Redd, 'The Abrahamic Covenant' in *Covenant Theology: Biblical, Theological, and Historical Perspectives*, eds. Guy Prentiss Waters, J. Nicholas Reid, and John R. Muether (Wheaton: Crossway, 2020), 138-141.

[53] Robert Letham, *Systematic Theology* (Wheaton: Crossway, 2019), 447.

Jacob (later named Israel) became the father of the twelve tribes of Israel. Jacob's sons end up in Egypt, where years later their descendants became slaves of the Egyptians. God then raised up Moses, who reminded the Israelites of God's promise to them for a land of their own in Canaan. God then set his people free from Egypt and they eventually settled in the Promised Land, under the leadership of Joshua. Thus God kept his promise to Abraham and fulfilled the first stage of this covenant – giving Abraham an heir, making his descendants numerous and giving his people the land of Canaan.[54]

Second Stage

Yet this was not the end of the fulfilment of the covenant, there was another stage to be fulfilled. The Promised Land was only a glimpse, a shadow, of a much greater reality to come. The realities themselves would only be fulfilled with the coming of Christ in the New Testament. How so?

Jesus bears the Covenant Curse: The rest of the Old Testament shows that all of Abraham's descendants continually broke covenant with God by their sin, rebellion and idolatry. The result was that they should have endured the penalty for breaking the covenant. What was that penalty? In the covenant making process in Genesis 15 we saw that it was death, symbolised by the slaughtered animals. Yet because only God passed through the dead animals, he alone promised to bear the curse for covenant breakers. This promise of God finds fulfilment in Christ. Galatians 3:13-14 says:

> *Christ redeemed us from the curse of the law by becoming a curse for us – for it is written, "Cursed is everyone who is hanged on a tree" – so that in Christ Jesus the blessing of Abraham might come to the Gentiles, so that we might receive the promised Spirit through faith.*

Like all the descendants of Abraham, we too are covenant breakers, we too have sinned and therefore deserve the curse of the covenant. But in Christ, whom the New Testament calls the "offspring of Abraham" (Gal. 3:16), God is faithful to his promise to bear the curse for those of us who have broken the covenant. How so? Jesus bore the curse for us by being

[54] Brown & Keele, *Sacred Bond*, 92-93.

slaughtered on the cross. His body was broken, his blood was shed, in our place. Instead of us having to bear that curse, God himself did, as he had promised he would to Abraham when he walked through the slaughtered animals as the covenant was established.

The Church is the Offspring of Abraham: God also fulfils his covenant with Abraham in a greater way in the New Testament in this way, Galatians 3:7-9 says:

> *Know then that it is those of faith who are the sons of Abraham. And the Scripture, foreseeing that God would justify the Gentiles by faith, preached the gospel beforehand to Abraham, saying, 'In you shall all the nations of the earth be blessed.' So then, those who are of faith are blessed along with Abraham, the man of faith.*

God's true people, his true offspring of Abraham, are not of a certain ethnic group, but are all those who as Abraham, by faith alone trust in Christ alone, and are justified by his work. This fulfils God's promise to Abraham that he would be the father of many nations, that through him the whole world would be blessed. The gospel would not remain exclusively with the nation of Israel, but, as God promised to Abraham, it would go to all the nations, as it is to be received by anyone who believes in Christ – both Jew and Gentile. This is why Galatians 3:29 says, "And if you are Christ's, then you are Abraham's offspring, heirs according to promise."

The New Creation is the True Promised Land: What then about the land? Was it not promised to Israel as an "everlasting possession" (Gen. 17:8)? How is that fulfilled on a greater level? The land of Canaan was just a type and shadow of something greater to come. The true Promised Land is the new heavens and the new earth. This is why Hebrews 11 says concerning the great Israelite leaders, they died *not having received the things promised*, but only having seen them from afar (11:13). "They desired a better country, that is a heavenly one. Therefore God is not ashamed to be called their God, for he has prepared for them a city" (11:16). This new promised city is indeed the new, heavenly Jerusalem. The Israelites, while having received the promised land of Canaan, in reality had not received the ultimate promise in their lifetime. The physical land was just a glimpse of something greater, the heavenly reality – the new heavens and new earth, which will indeed be the everlasting possession of all Abraham's offspring.[55] This is why Romans 4:13 says that the promise to Abraham and his offspring was that he would be "the heir of the world."

Implications of the Abrahamic Covenant

There is Only One People of God

God has not made two parallel covenants that run simultaneously with each other – one covenant with Israel and another with the church. The church is the fulfilment of Israel, she is the new Israel; who has been grafted into Israel, as Romans 11:17 tells us. Therefore the church is the same covenant community that God began in Genesis 3:15. We are descended from the seed of the woman, the seed of Abraham, all part of the one continuing covenant of grace.

Similarly, God has no "favoured nation" anywhere on earth. In the light of the truth of the covenant of grace, it is completely illegitimate for nations, cultural, racial groups, or even social classes to claim that God has made a special covenant with them and that they are some sort of a "chosen people". God's only chosen people is his church, for which he bled and died, ransoming them out of "every tribe and language and people and nation" (Rev. 5:9).

Children form part of the Covenant Community

Children were included in God's covenant with Abraham, they received the sign of the covenant, circumcision, as babies. The reason for this was that the covenant promise was not only made to Abraham, but also to his children, his offspring after him (Gen. 17:7). Because of the continuity of the covenant of grace from the Old Testament through to the New Testament, we see that children in the New Testament are likewise included in the new covenant community. However, the sign of the covenant changes in the new covenant administration of the covenant of grace from circumcision to baptism (Col. 2:11-12). This is because circumcision involves the shedding of blood and was only performed on males. In the

---

55 Brown & Keele, *Sacred Bond*, 93-94.

new covenant, Jesus has shed his blood on our behalf, therefore no more blood is required to be shed. The new covenant promise of the Spirit is more inclusive than the old, as it is for both males and females (Joel 2:28), therefore both males and females receive baptism. The promises of the new covenant blessings are intended not only for adults, but their children too, as was the case in the Abrahamic covenant. This is why Peter, preaching at Pentecost, proclaims concerning the new covenant promise of the gospel, echoes the same promise of the Abrahamic covenant in Genesis 17:7, "For the promise is for you *and for your children* and for all who are far off, everyone whom the Lord our God calls to himself" (Acts 2:39) (emphasis mine). This points us to the truth that through the covenant of grace, God does not only deal with us as individuals, but also as "organic wholes, including families and generations."[56] Therefore it is entirely appropriate that children of parents in the covenant community be baptised, as they are included in the covenant of grace and God desires that they too share in the blessings of the covenant.[57] This is precisely why the Heidelberg Catechism, Q & A 74, states:

> *Q. Should infants also be baptised?*
>
> *A. Yes. Infants as well as adults are included in God's covenant and people, and they, no less than adults, are promised deliverance from sin through Christ's blood and the Holy Spirit who produces faith. Therefore, by baptism, the sign of the covenant, they too should be incorporated into the Christian church and distinguished from the children of unbelievers. This was done in the Old Testament by circumcision, which was replaced in the New Testament by baptism.*

Grace for all Nations

Through God's covenant with Abraham, we see that the gospel is meant for all nations. God's promise to Abraham was that his offspring would be a light to all the nations. The gospel was never meant to stay with one ethnic group, or belong to one race or culture. It is not exclusive, and God's people are not to be insular. All the nations must hear the good news of grace

---

56 Bavinck, *Reformed Dogmatics*, vol. 3, 196.

57 Brown & Keele, *Sacred Bond*, 95-96.

through Jesus Christ. This means that the church must go to all nations and proclaim the gospel.

God's Covenant Promise is True

We can have absolute confidence in God's promise to us to grant us eternity with him in the new creation, the heavenly Jerusalem. We know this because he has fulfilled all the other promises of the covenant: granting a son of promise to Abraham, making many nations from him and giving the land to Israel in the Old Testament. Therefore we can be encouraged that the promise of the new creation is our glorious inheritance. We can look forward to the Day when the covenant is fulfilled, when we will dwell face to face for all eternity with our Lord, as Revelation 21:3 tells us: "Behold the dwelling place of God is with man. He will dwell with them, and they will be his people, and God himself will be with them as their God."

Conclusion

Ultimately God's covenant with Abraham, as an administration of the covenant of grace, points to Christ's work of salvation: forgiveness of sins and justification through faith alone. Romans 4:1-8 declares:

> *What then shall we say was gained by Abraham, our forefather according to the flesh? For if Abraham was justified by works, he has something to boast about, but not before God. For what does the Scripture say? "Abraham believed God, and it was counted to him as righteousness." Now to the one who works, his wages are not counted as a gift but as his due. And to the one who does not work but believes in him who justifies the ungodly, his faith is counted as righteousness, just as David also speaks of the blessing of the one to whom God counts righteousness apart from works:*
>
> *"Blessed are those whose lawless deeds are forgiven, and whose sins are covered; blessed is the man against whom the Lord will not count his sin."*

Abraham believed God, and it was counted to him as righteousness (Gen. 15:6). God blessed Abraham and justified him on the basis of faith and not because of his works. In the same way, we are not made right with God because of our works. Instead, like Abraham, it is "the one who does *not work* but *believes in him* who justifies the ungodly" (Rom. 4:5) (emphasis mine), he is the one who is justified, forgiven of his sins and counted with the righteousness of Christ as gift of grace.

Discussion Questions

1. What were the central promises of the covenant that God made with Abraham?
2. How was Abraham made right with God?
3. How is the promise of the land as an "everlasting possession" to Abraham and his offspring ultimately fulfilled?
4. How does the covenant-making ceremony in Genesis 15 point us to Christ and his work on the cross?
5. How is it that Christians are now considered children of Abraham? What significance does this have in terms of how God deals with his people? Is it legitimate for nations to claim that God has made a special covenant with them?
6. Make the case for infant baptism. Why is this practice biblically legitimate in the light of the Abrahamic covenant?

6 | The Mosaic Covenant

Setting the Scene

In the previous chapter, we saw that through the Abrahamic covenant God promised to multiply the descendants of Abraham into a great nation, and give this nation of Israel a land of their own. As biblical history continues to unfold, we see that Abraham's grandson, Jacob (later renamed, Israel), and his twelve sons and their families, end up in Egypt because of a series of events related to Jacob's son, Joseph (Gen. 37-50). At first the Israelites (descendants of Israel), found favour under Pharaoh and flourished in Egypt. However, as they remained there for some four hundred years, the Egyptians began to oppress and enslave them.

In the midst of this oppression, God raised up a deliverer for his people, an Israelite named Moses. God appeared to him in the burning bush in Exodus 3, revealed his personal name, Yahweh, to him, and said that he has seen the oppression of his people Israel (Ex. 3:7, 14). He also said that he has not forgotten the covenant promises that he made to his people through the Abrahamic covenant, to grant them a Promised Land of their own, "to bring them... to a good and broad land, a land flowing with milk and honey..." (Ex. 3:8).

God used Moses to deliver his people out of bondage and slavery in Egypt, and into this Promised Land which he had promised Abraham. Through a series of ten plagues, God defeated the gods of Egypt, which led to Pharaoh allowing the Israelites to flee. But Pharaoh soon changed his mind and sent his army in pursuit of the Israelites. In a display of God's power and might as Israel's King, he opened up the waters of the Red Sea that blocked Israel from escaping Pharaoh's army, and allowed them to escape the oppression of Egypt. Meanwhile, Pharaoh and his army were drowned in the waters of the Sea as they tried to follow them. God saved his people by his mighty hand and outstretched arm, and brought them to Mount Sinai, where he made another covenant with them, through Moses.

It was here, on Mount Sinai, that the Mosaic covenant was made between God and Israel. The heart of the covenant was given in the form of the Ten Commandments (Ex. 20:1-17), and subsequently the entire law (Torah) of Israel – the terms of the covenant. The complete law is found in Exodus, Leviticus, Numbers and Deuteronomy. In all, there are said to be 613 laws contained in the Law of Moses.

The covenant was then ratified in Exodus 24. Still at Mount Sinai, Moses read the words of the covenant to the people of Israel. Exodus 24:3 says that immediately after this, "all the people answered with one voice and said, "All the words that the Lord has spoken we will do." Israel swore an oath before God to obey the terms of the covenant. The oath was sealed by Moses building an altar, representing God, and twelve pillars, representing Israel's twelve tribes (24:4). Burnt offerings were made and oxen were sacrificed to God. The blood from the oxen, representing both life (cleansing from sin) and death (the penalty for breaking the covenant), was collected and half of it was thrown upon the altar, symbolically upon God himself. Like God taking upon himself the obligation to keep the Abrahamic covenant in Genesis 15 by passing through the carcasses; he promised to keep his oath of the covenant.[58]

Moses then threw the rest of the blood upon the people. In verse 8, he declared, "Behold the blood of the covenant that the Lord has made with you in accordance with all these words." The covenant ceremony was concluded with a covenant meal as Moses, Aaron and the seventy elders of Israel went up onto Mount Sinai and ate and drank before the presence of God (24:9-10). Thus both God and Israel took an oath to keep this covenant. The ratification of the covenant highlights the works element in the covenant: Israel promised to obey the words of the covenant. Failure to do so will result in death.[59]

The purpose of this law covenant was to govern Israel's life in the Promised Land that God was about to give them. If Israel were to obey these laws, God promised to bless and protect them in the land. If they were to disobey, God promised to curse them and ultimately expel them

---

[58] Brown & Keele, *Sacred Bond*, 109.

[59] Brown & Keele, *Sacred Bond*, 109-110.

from the land. This is why Leviticus 18:4-5 declares, "You shall follow my rules and keep my statutes and walk in them. I am the Lord your God. You shall therefore keep my statutes and my rules; if a person does them, he shall live by them: I am the Lord."

Grace or Law?

Is the Mosaic covenant a covenant of grace or law? It is clear that there is grace in the Mosaic covenant. God graciously delivered Israel out of slavery in Egypt. He defeated their enemies and brought them into a new land. It was all his work, and Israel received it freely as a gift of grace. This is essentially what the prologue of the Ten Commandments declares (Ex. 20:1-2).

Further, the entire sacrificial system that makes up the Mosaic covenant is gracious in nature. Instead of Israel having to bear the penalty of death for their sins, God allowed animals to be sacrificed for the sins of the people instead. These sacrifices, though insufficient to effectively deal with sin, as they had to be repeated year after year (Heb. 10:1-4), foreshadow the perfect sacrifice of Christ on the cross, where he definitively atoned for the sins of his people.

So because of this, we affirm that the Mosaic covenant, like the Abrahamic covenant, is an administration of the covenant of grace.[60] God saved his people by grace, giving them the Promised Land as a gift. And as we shall soon see, he also gave Israel the law with the purpose that they would trust in Christ for salvation, showing them that only his perfect righteousness could save sinners.

At the same time, it is also clear that the Mosaic covenant is a covenant of law. In order to enjoy God's blessing and protection in the Promised Land, Israel must obey the law. There are terms to the covenant that must be obeyed. If they fail to obey them, they will be cursed and be expelled from the land. There are blessings for obedience and curses for disobedience (Deut. 28:1-68).

Does this not sound familiar? Indeed it does. The Mosaic covenant, like the original covenant of works with Adam, contains a works principle. It

[60] Westminster Confession of Faith 7.4-5.

resembles the covenant of works in important respects. But this time the works principle is not with Adam, but instead with Israel. This is why the Westminster Confession of Faith 19.2 states that the moral "law, after [Adam's] fall, continued to be a perfect rule of righteousness; and, as such was delivered by God upon Mount Sinai, in ten commandments..."

In the covenant of works that God made with Adam, he promised abundant life in the Garden of Eden for his obedience. Similarly, in the Mosaic covenant that God made with Israel, he promised abundant life in another "garden" – the Promised Land – if they obeyed. With Adam, God promised to expel them from the Garden to live a cursed existence if they disobeyed. With Israel, God promised to expel them from the Promised Land if they disobeyed. There is clearly a works principle that is common to both covenants.

Both Adam and Israel failed to fulfil their side of the covenant due to their disobedience. Through this, they were made to realise that they could not earn heaven on their own. Both covenants therefore show that it is impossible for fallen man to perfectly keep the law. Instead, they point us to the only Righteous One who has perfectly obeyed the law, Jesus Christ. This is why Galatians 3:24 says, "So then, the law was our guardian until Christ came, in order that we might be justified by faith."

There is an important difference, though, between the covenant of works and Mosaic covenant. As we saw in chapter 2, if Adam had perfectly obeyed the covenant of works, he would have earned everlasting life. Yet this is not so with Israel in the Mosaic covenant. Israel was in no way saved by obedience to the covenant. Israel was elected and saved for everlasting life sovereignly by God, purely as an act of grace, which she received by faith. Instead, Israel's obedience to the Mosaic covenant only merited temporal blessing and life in the Promised Land. This, after all, was only a picture, a glimpse, of the ultimate Promised Land, heaven itself.

We can therefore see both grace and law in the Mosaic covenant. It is an administration of the one covenant of grace that stretches across redemptive history, as it points to Christ and his salvation. Yet what makes the Mosaic covenant distinctive among the various administrations of the covenant of grace is this works principle that made temporal blessing contingent on covenant loyalty. While Israel is not saved by works (she is saved by grace through faith according to the Abrahamic covenant), Israel's possession of the land is conditioned on its covenantal obedience.[61]

The Three-fold Division of the Law

One main purpose of the Mosaic covenant was to put in place a legal framework for the nation of Israel when they lived in the Promised Land. In other words, the law of Moses was specifically given for the theocracy of Israel. Since New Testament times, Christians have understood some distinction within the law. This is clear in Acts 15, when the early church met to discuss the relationship of law-keeping to the gospel in Jerusalem. Later on in church history, a three-fold distinction of the law was made: ceremonial, civil and moral. This too is how the Westminster Confession of Faith categorises the law.[62] It is really important to understand these distinctions, as a failure to do so leads to confusion as to what parts of the law are relevant for the Christian life. For example, the law forbids the eating of shellfish (Lev. 11:12), as well as homosexuality (Lev. 18:22). Are Christians being inconsistent then, when we affirm the sinfulness of homosexuality, yet eat shellfish? A correct understanding of the three-fold division of the law will help us avoid confusion in this regard.

Ceremonial: Those parts of the law concerned with worship of the Israelites, the sacrificial system, and the shedding blood of animals to atone for Israel's sin. It also includes the various dietary laws which were a way for Israel to distinguish herself from the surrounding pagan nations. They showed what was considered to be "clean" and "unclean."

---

[61] J. Nicholas Reid, 'The Mosaic Covenant' in *Covenant Theology: Biblical, Theological, and Historical Perspectives*, eds. Guy Prentiss Waters, J. Nicholas Reid, and John R. Muether (Wheaton: Crossway, 2020), 166-167; Kline, *Kingdom Prologue*, 109; Bryan D. Estelle, J.V. Fesko and David VanDrunen, 'Introduction' in *The Law is not of Faith: Essays on Works and Grace in the Mosaic Covenant*, eds. Bryan D. Estelle, J.V. Fesko and David VanDrunen, (Phillipsburg: P&R Publishing, 2009), 11-14; Brenton C. Ferry, 'Works in the Mosaic Covenant: A Reformed Taxonomy' in *The Law is not of Faith: Essays on Works and Grace in the Mosaic Covenant*, eds. Bryan D. Estelle, J.V. Fesko and David VanDrunen, (Phillipsburg: P&R Publishing, 2009), 90-96.

[62] Westminster Confession of Faith 19.

Civil: Those parts of the law which showed how Israel was to live in the Promised Land. These laws were specific to civil functioning of the theocracy. Examples of civil laws include the agricultural practices for Israel, all the judicial laws, aspects of the Sabbath regulations, and instructions on how to treat the poor and foreigners.

Moral: The moral law is summed up in the Ten Commandments. These are the laws concerning human behaviour, sexual ethic and morality, in relation to God and fellow man.

Deuteronomy 28, which was recorded at the end of the giving of the law, shows us that the nature of this covenant was conditional. "If you obey then I will bless you, if you will not obey then I will curse you..." The covenant blessings included: a blessed existence within the Promised Land, the land will yield fruit, an increase in herds, God's promise to defeat any enemies, abundance and prosperity. The covenant curses included: fruitlessness, disease, defeat in battle, sickness and ultimately exile, the loss of the land.

Ultimately Israel was unable to keep the law, this covenant. She failed in every respect – this is the sad story of Israel, characterised by corrupt rulers, injustices, immorality, false worship and idolatry. She continually broke the law. God sent the prophets to Israel to remind them of the covenant that he had made with them and that they were breaking it. Despite these many warnings, they continued in their sin and rebellion. Eventually because of Israel's breaking of the covenant, God cursed Israel (as he said he would if they disobeyed) and exiled them to Assyria and Babylon. They were unable to keep this covenant, they broke it, showing the need for a new covenant and showing up their inability to obey the law on their own. This looks forward to the new covenant that God promised would come in Jeremiah 31:31-34, when he would write the law in their hearts. Through the Mosaic covenant, Israel was being pointed ultimately to Christ who was the only one able to fulfil the law and whose sacrifice would secure complete and everlasting forgiveness of sins.

Jesus fulfils the Mosaic covenant

How is Jesus able to fulfil this covenant?

fulfils the ceremonial law: Jesus' death on the cross was a once for all (Heb. 9:12) which is sufficient to take away all the sins of God's people, past, present and future. No further sacrifices are needed; the blood of ox and bulls is redundant. Jesus has fulfilled the ceremonial aspect of the law by his atoning death on the cross. All the Old Testament sacrificial laws point to the one perfect sacrifice that was to come in Jesus.

The dietary laws that set Israel apart from the nations have been fulfilled and ended in Christ. Mark 7:18–19, "[Jesus] said to them ... 'Do you not see that whatever goes into a person from outside cannot defile him?' ... (Thus he declared all foods clean.)." This is why Christians are no longer bound to obey the dietary laws of the old covenant.

Jesus fulfils the civil law: There is no longer a theocracy, the Old Testament nation of Israel no longer exists. In fact, Jesus himself is the new Israel. He succeeded and obeyed the law, where the nation of Israel failed. Hence, in Christ, the civil law is fulfilled.

Further, God's people do not live in only one country any more. Jesus' people are now the church, and the church forms part of God's spiritual kingdom. Therefore those civil laws that applied to Israel living in the Promised Land no longer apply to us. This does not mean that we cannot glean principles from them and apply them today, for example, timeless ideas of justice and treatment of the poor and the foreigner are applicable to us.[63]

Because Christ has fulfilled the civil law, this means that we are to be subject to the political authority which the Lord has placed over us. This is why *Romans 13:1* says, "Let every person be subject to the governing authorities. For there is no authority except from God, and those that exist have been instituted by God." In the new covenant there is a distinction between the church and state, as we are no longer under a theocracy.[64]

Jesus fulfils the moral law: Jesus lived the perfectly obedient life on earth – he never sinned (1 Pet. 2:22). He therefore kept the whole moral law, and his flawless righteousness is imputed—credited—to us by grace through faith (Phil. 3:9).

---

[63] Belgic Confession 25.

[64] Westminster Confession of Faith 23.3, 31.4.

Are Christians bound to keep the Law?

Does the law then have any relevance or bearing for Christians? Throughout church history, there have been two broad tendencies in this regard. The first is a tendency toward legalism. Legalists teach that one is saved through law keeping. It is said that God accepts us on the merit of our good works and obedience to the law. The Judaizers in the early church were legalists, and were defeated at the Jerusalem Council in Acts 15. Galatians 3:10-12 declares:

> *For all who rely on works of the law are under a curse; for it is written, "Cursed be everyone who does not abide by all things written in the Book of the Law, and do them." Now it is evident that no one is justified before God by the law, for "The righteous shall live by faith." But the law is not of faith, rather "The one who does them shall live by them."*

It is clear that our salvation is not earned by our obedience to the law. Obedience to the law alone will never grant us saving grace, nor can it ever offer us a solution out of the misery of our sinful state. Instead it just leaves sinners under a curse because they will always fall short of the righteousness that the law demands.[65]

The second tendency is toward antinomianism. Antinomianism completely rejects any need for the law. It teaches that since we are under grace, the law is no longer necessary to regulate our conduct. According to antinomians, not only the ceremonial and civil law, but also the moral law expressed in the Ten Commandments was only for those under the old covenant; so we are to absolutely disregard it. Like legalism, antinomianism too was rejected by the apostles in the New Testament. Romans 7:12 says, "So the law is holy, and the commandment is holy and righteous and good." It is also clear to us that utter disregard for the law, living as we see fit, is incompatible with biblical faith.

What then is the role of the law in the life of a Christian? Firstly, we need to be clear that Jesus perfectly fulfilled and obeyed the Mosaic covenant, in which is contained the law. Therefore, if we are in Christ, we are no longer under the law, but under grace (Rom. 6:14, 7:6).

---

[65] Canons of Dort III & IV.5.

What does it mean to no longer be under the law? This means that our own obedience to the law can never earn us everlasting life. Because Jesus has completely obeyed the law, he is the only Righteous One, and therefore only he has earned everlasting life. If we are in Christ, he imputes to us his perfect righteousness, covering our own unrighteousness (as none of us can keep the law perfectly). "For as by one man's disobedience many were made sinners, so by one man's obedience many will be made righteous" (Rom. 5:19). We have been released from the burden of having to obey the whole law. Instead Christ has fulfilled this burden on our behalf, and counts his righteousness to us as a result.

So does this mean that we do not need to pay any attention whatsoever to the law? Not at all! We are no longer "under the law" meaning that obedience to the law does not save us, Christ having fulfilled it. Yet Christians are still bound to obey the moral law, which is summed up in the Ten Commandments.[66] Those commandments reveal what it means to love our neighbour (Rom. 13:9-10), and by God's Spirit this law's righteous requirement is fulfilled in us (Rom. 8:4).

The Three-fold Use of the Law

Calvin helpfully identified three ways the law is useful for the Christian (otherwise known as the three-fold use of the law). The first use of the law is that it reveals our sin, and points us to our need for a Saviour. It is also called the pedagogical use of the law. In this way, the law is our "schoolmaster" unto Christ (Gal. 3:24) (Greek = *paidagōgos*). We only know that gossip, jealousy, drunkenness, murder, envy, theft and sexual immorality are sins because of the law. This is why Romans 7:7 says, "If it had not been for the law, I would not have known sin." The law leads to confession, repentance of our sins and leads us to trust instead in Christ for salvation.

The second use of the law is that it acts as a restraint against evil. This is also called the civil use of the law. The threat of punishment under the law is used in societies throughout the world, in order to restrain human sin. Paul describes the law acting in this regard in Romans 13:1-7.

---

[66] Belgic Confession 25; Westminster Confession of Faith 19.5.

The third use of the law is that it is our guide unto holy living. This is also called the didactical use of the law. In this way, the law shows us the will of God for our lives, the best way to live a life that glorifies and pleases God. Jesus said in John 14:15, "If you love me, keep my commandments." We are only able to keep his commandments by the work of the Holy Spirit in our lives.[67]

Conclusion

Are Christians bound by the Mosaic covenant? Are we still under the law? No, not in the sense that Adam and Israel were under the law (Rom. 7:6, Gal. 3:19). We are not made righteous by obeying the law, nor are we saved by law-keeping. Christ has done that on our behalf. We are saved by Christ's obedience to the law, not our own. Yet this does not mean that the law is abolished. This is why Jesus says, "Do not think that I have come to abolish the Law or the Prophets; I have not come to abolish them but to fulfil them" (Matt. 5:17). Though we are not saved by law-keeping, Christians are most certainly bound to keep the moral law, as it is our guide to holy living and it brings us conviction of our sins and shows up our continual need for a Saviour from our sins, the only Righteous One, Jesus Christ.

[67] John Calvin. *Institutes of the Christian Religion*, trans. Lewis Ford Battles, ed. John T. McNeill, (Philadelphia: Westminster John Knox, 1960), 2.7.1-17; Andrew A. Woolsey, *Unity and Continuity in Covenantal Thought: A Study in the Reformed Tradition to the Westminster Assembly* (Grand Rapids: Reformation Heritage Books, 2012), 296-305; Joel R. Beeke & Mark Jones, *A Puritan Theology: Doctrine for Life* (Grand Rapids: Reformation Heritage Books, 2012), 283-284.

Discussion Questions

1. What was the purpose of the Mosaic covenant?
2. Explain how the Mosaic covenant is an administration of the covenant of grace.
3. Explain the significance of the works principle in the Mosaic covenant.
4. What is the three-fold division of the law? How did Jesus fulfil each division of the law? Why is this division of the law so important for us to understand?
5. In what way are Christians still bound to keep the law? How do we reconcile continued obedience to the law with the truth that we have been saved by grace alone?
6. Explain Calvin's three-fold use of the law. How do you find this to be helpful for the Christian life?

7 | The Davidic Covenant

Setting the Scene

In the previous chapter, we saw that Moses received the law from the Lord, on Mount Sinai, in preparation for Israel's life in the Promised Land. Moses then led the nation of Israel through the wilderness until bringing them to Mount Nebo, which overlooked the Promised Land, where he died. It was his successor, Joshua, who led Israel into the Promised Land, to possess it.

Some five hundred years later, a young shepherd boy in Israel, named David, rose to fame after he slayed the Philistine giant, Goliath, while Saul was still on the throne. Eventually when he succeeded Saul as king, it was under his reign that Israel grew into a great nation. He wrote many of the psalms, which show us his heart for worshipping God. In fact, God himself called him, "a man after his own heart" (1 Sam. 13:14). He would be regarded as one of Israel's finest kings.

Almost everything we know about David in the Bible is about his life as king. David is first introduced to us in 1 Samuel 16, where the prophet Samuel went to Jesse's household to anoint the next king of Israel. God led Samuel to anoint Jesse's youngest son, David, as Israel's next king. From that moment on, David was God's chosen king for Israel, even though Saul remained king for a while. Eventually when Saul died, David took over from him and ruled over Israel for the rest of his life.

What is the Davidic Covenant?

The Davidic covenant is a covenant that God made with King David that established his dynasty in Israel. Through the covenant, God promised David that his descendants would play an important part in the redemption of his people. God promised that one of David's descendants would save Israel from their enemies. God's promise in Genesis 3:15, that a seed of the woman will crush the head of the serpent, is developed further here. David was a descendant of Eve, and God promised him through this covenant that someone from his line, a Messiah (anointed one), will reign forever on his throne, establishing an everlasting kingdom.[68]

Biblical Evidence for the Davidic Covenant

2 Samuel 7

This is the key text for the Davidic covenant. Some context: a few chapters earlier (2 Sam. 5), David succeeded Saul as Israel's king. One of his first acts as king was to order that the Ark of the Covenant (where God's presence dwelt) be brought into Jerusalem, showing his primary concern was the worship of God.

Up until that point the Ark had been kept in a tent. But in chapter 7, David decided that he must build a house for God. In verses 2-3, David said to the prophet Nathan, "See now, I dwell in a house of cedar, but the ark of God dwells in a tent." And Nathan said to the king, "Go, do all that is in your heart, for the LORD is with you."

Then God spoke to Nathan the prophet and through him, made a covenant with David. God promised David that he will make his name great (7:9), under his reign, Israel shall have peace (7:10-11), and that though David wants to build God a house, God actually does not need a house to live in. We can note too the parallel verse in 1 Chronicles 17:4, "It is not you who will build me a house to dwell in. For I have not lived in a house since I was brought up to Israel..." Instead God will build David a house (7:11). This "house" is not a physical structure as David intends to build for God, but it is instead a dynasty, a kingdom. It will be built through his offspring; God will also establish the throne of David, his kingdom forever (7:13-14). God will be to David as a father, and David as his son (7:14). God's steadfast, covenantal love (Hebrew = *hesed*), will never depart from him (7:15). The nature of God's covenant with David is that David's kingdom and his throne will be established forever by God(7:16).[69]

Unconditional Nature of the Covenant: It is clear here that the first aspect of this covenant is unconditional: God promised to fulfil the terms unilaterally,

---

68 Brown & Keele, *Sacred Bond*, 122-123.

69 Brown & Keele, *Sacred Bond*, 123-125.

and this is not dependent on David's or David's sons' obedience. God's love will be upon David and David's son to establish his house, his kingdom and the throne forever. Nothing can stop God achieving this. The unconditional nature of the covenant is confirmed in Psalm 89:34-37:

> *I will not violate my covenant or alter the word that went forth from my lips. Once for all I have sworn by my holiness; I will not lie to David. His offspring shall endure for ever, his throne as long as the sun before me. Like the moon it shall be established forever, a faithful witness in the skies.*

We see here that this is a future promise. It will not be fulfilled in David, but through his offspring, who "shall endure for ever" (89:36). It will be his offspring who establish his kingdom eternally. Who then is David's offspring? One can assume that it is Solomon, David's son.

Conditional Nature of the Covenant: It is also clear that the second aspect of the covenant is conditional. David's son is required to do something in order to receive the eternal throne. In verse 13 it says, "He shall build a house for my name, and I will establish the throne of his kingdom for ever." God's establishment of David's throne depends on David's son's building of the house. Now what is in mind here is not just the actual temple in Jerusalem, which Solomon ended up building. David was not able to build the temple, as he was a man of war. However, his son, Solomon (Hebrew = *Šəlōmō*, from the root word, *šalōm*, meaning peace) was a man of peace, so he was able to do it. God's "house" is not only the temple, but also the people of God. This is because God's house implicitly includes God's people (7:7) and God's house is directly linked to his kingdom. Therefore the work of David's son is not only to build the temple in Jerusalem, but also includes God's people and his kingdom. The house is also to be for God's name (7:13). The purpose of the house is to honour and glorify God. How does one do this? Obey God's Word. This is why God promises to discipline David's son in verse 14 when he strays from God's commandments. The conditional element in the Davidic covenant is therefore that David's son must be obedient to God in his building of God's house, his kingdom.[70]

[70] Brown & Keele, *Sacred Bond*, 127.

1 Kings 9

We can see more of the conditional aspect of the Davidic covenant in this passage. Here we see that now David's son, Solomon, has succeeded David as Israel's king. Initially Solomon began his reign well. He asked God for wisdom to lead Israel and distinguish between good and evil (1 Kin. 3:9). He ruled with wisdom and justice and the result was that the nation prospered. Israel reached its zenith in terms of political and economic power. Each man lived under his vine and fig tree, which is biblical language to indicate that everyone enjoyed prosperity. The nation also lived in peace. Solomon built the temple in Jerusalem that his father wanted to build, in order to house the Ark of the Covenant. When the Ark was brought into the completed temple, God's glory filled the temple. It is becoming increasingly clear that God's promise to David has now been fulfilled. 1 Kings 8:20 says, "Now the Lord has fulfilled his promise that he made. For I have risen in the place of David my father, and sit on the throne of Israel, as the Lord promised, and I have built the house for the name of the Lord, the God of Israel."

Yet even though this has been fulfilled in one sense, God goes on to say to Solomon in 1 Kings 9:4-5 that, "if you will walk before me...doing according to all that I have commanded you, and keeping my statutes and my rules, then I will establish your royal throne over Israel forever, as I promised David."

So on the one hand God's promise to David is fulfilled in Solomon in that he has built God a house, the temple; and he as David's son now sits on the throne. Yet on the other hand, God says that it is only if Solomon continues in his obedience to him that will ensure that his throne will be everlasting.

We can see clearly the unconditional and conditional elements of the covenant come together with Solomon. The Davidic dynasty will continue regardless because God has promised it so. Yet only an obedient, righteous son of David will receive the throne eternally.

If we look at the rest of Solomon's life, we see a tragic story unfold. He married seven hundred women, had another three hundred concubines (1 Kin. 11:3). He intermarried with the surrounding pagan nations which

God had forbidden. These women then led him to worship their false gods, and he goes astray (1 Kin. 11:3-5). He disobeyed God and therefore showed that he was not the righteous son of David that was promised, and does not stay on the throne eternally. First Kings 11:6, laments that, "Solomon did what was evil in the sight of the LORD and did not wholly follow the LORD, as David his father had done." Yet God keeps him on the throne for a time because he promised to build David's dynasty regardless.

After Solomon, the nation of Israel divides in two: the northern kingdom of Israel and southern kingdom of Judah. Their history is recorded in the books of 1 and 2 Kings and 1 and 2 Chronicles. Here we see how David and Solomon's descendants fared in ruling God's people. Most of the kings were atrocious leaders, they led people into idolatry, false worship, disobedience, immorality and injustice. Once in a while there arose a good king, but the vast majority were terrible. Yet God is faithful to the covenant he made with David. David's line is preserved in the southern kingdom of Judah. Despite the numerous evil kings, God continues David's line by disciplining the evil kings and replacing them with another king until the truly righteous son arises. God will never break his covenant to the house of David, but it is only the righteous son of David who will gain the everlasting throne.[71]

Psalm 2

We can see elements of the Davidic covenant present in this psalm. Psalm 2 celebrates the anointing of a new Davidic king. Verse 2 talks about "the Lord and his Anointed." The Hebrew for "Anointed" is *mašîyah* or Messiah. Already, we can see the promise of God to send an anointed one, a Messiah, a king in the line of David. Verse 6 says, "I have set my king on Zion, my holy hill." Here God makes the connection between his kingship and the kingship of David's house. Then God declares to the newly anointed king, "You are my son; today I have begotten you." (2:7) – making a connection between God's promise to David that he will be like a father to him and his sons, and the king will be his son.[72]

---

[71] Brown & Keele, *Sacred Bond*, 127-130.

[72] Brown & Keele, *Sacred Bond*, 130; O. Palmer Robertson, *The Christ of the Covenants* (Phillipsburg: P&R Publishers, 1980), 233-234.

Psalm 16

David wrote this psalm, and verse 10 says, "For you will not abandon my soul to Sheol, or let your holy one see corruption." David is looking forward to the righteous son that God has promised him, a son that will not be abandoned to the dead or rot in the grave. In Acts 2:27 when Peter is preaching at Pentecost, he proclaims that Jesus is the fulfilment of this psalm. David and his other sons are dead in the grave, yet Jesus, the true son of David, has been raised from the dead and now reigns on David's throne eternally.[73]

The New Testament

By the time Jesus was born, the Jews were still waiting for God to fulfil his promise to send them a ruler, a son of David, the Messiah, who would rule justly and in righteousness and whose throne would last forever. He would make his people holy, establishing the true temple of God and fully keep God's law. The son of David would crush all Israel's enemies and would establish peace, righteousness and justice in his rule. This is why the first verse of the New Testament calls Jesus Christ "the son of David, the son of Abraham" (Matt. 1:1). The genealogies prove that Jesus is descended from David, who is in turn descended from Abraham, who is in turn descended from Adam and Eve. So here is the fulfilment of Genesis 3:15, the seed of the woman coming to crush the head of the serpent. Jesus, the seed of Eve, the true son of David, is the promised Messiah.

Similarly, the angel Gabriel announced to the virgin Mary concerning the son she would conceive, "He will be great and will be called the Son of the Most High. And the Lord God will give to him the throne of his father David, and he will reign over the house of Jacob forever, and of his kingdom there will be no end" (Luke 1:32-33).

Romans 1:1-4 also announces that Jesus is a descendant of David: "the gospel of God, which he promised beforehand through his prophets in the holy Scriptures, concerning his Son, who was descended from David according to the flesh and was declared to be the Son of God in power according to the Spirit of holiness by his resurrection from the dead, Jesus Christ our Lord."

---

[73] Brown & Keele, *Sacred Bond*, 130-131.

Jesus came as the greater son of David to fulfil the Davidic covenant by building a house for God's name. The temple Jesus built was not a physical temple, like Solomon's, but the true temple is spiritual and eternal. It is where God's presence dwells forever, his church. This is why Jesus told the Samaritan woman in John 4:23 that his people would no longer worship God in the temple in Jerusalem, but instead "in Spirit and truth." God's true temple that Jesus built is the church, and now the Holy Spirit tabernacles among God's people who are the church (1 Cor. 3:16-17).

When Jesus enters Jerusalem on a donkey the week before his crucifixion, the crowds welcome him and recognise him as the promised son of David as they exclaim, "Hosanna! Blessed is he who comes in the name of the Lord! Blessed is the coming kingdom of our father David! Hosanna in the highest!" (Mark 11:9).[74]

Conclusion

Jesus reigns forever on the throne of David, at the right hand of the Father in all eternity. God's promise to David of an eternal kingdom and an eternal house carrying his name is finally fulfilled in Christ.

Discussion Questions

1. How is the Davidic covenant an expression of the covenant of grace? In what way does it anticipate the coming of the seed of the woman?
2. What are the central promises of the Davidic covenant?
3. In what ways is the Davidic covenant both conditional and unconditional? Why is this significant?
4. How is Jesus the fulfilment of the Davidic covenant promises?
5. How is the kingship of Christ, in the light of the Davidic covenant promises, a great comfort to you?

---

[74] Brown & Keele, *Sacred Bond*, 131-132.

8 | The New Covenant

Setting the Scene

We saw in the previous chapter that it looked as if Solomon would fulfil the covenant promises made to his father, David. David's son reigned on his father's throne: he had built a magnificent temple for God and his reign over Israel was marked by huge blessing and abundance for the whole nation (1 Kin. 4:20-34). Yet as great as Solomon was, in his later life he was led astray by his many wives into idolatry. He did not walk faithfully before the Lord as his father had done, and therefore did not fulfil the conditional side of the Davidic covenant.

We also saw that the kingdom of Israel after Solomon split in two and both kingdoms, Israel and Judah, ruled by successively bad kings, continued on a wayward path of disobedience and idolatry. King after king defied God and led the people in breaking the Mosaic covenant, the very laws God had given Israel for living a blessed life within the Promised Land.

At this time, God raised up the prophets who confronted the kings of Israel and Judah. They reminded them of the terms of the Mosaic covenant, that God would bless them in the land if they obeyed, or curse them if they disobeyed. They warned the kings that if they continued to disobey God instead of repenting, God would bring judgement upon the nation and send the people into exile.

Yet the prophets also brought hope. They prophesied a time when God would send his promised Messiah, the promised seed of the woman who would crush the head of the serpent. Although the people had broken the Mosaic covenant through their continued disobedience, God had not forgotten his unconditional promises to Israel through the Abrahamic covenant of grace, that he would always be their God and they his people. It would be through the coming of the Messiah and by the power of the Holy Spirit that God would fulfil this promise. It is into this setting that the prophet Jeremiah prophesies concerning the new covenant in Jeremiah 31:31-34:

> *Behold, the days are coming, declares the Lord, when I will make a new covenant with the house of Israel and the house of Judah, not like the covenant that I made with their fathers on the day when I took them by the hand to bring them out of the land of Egypt, my covenant that they broke, though I was their husband, declares the Lord. For this is the covenant that I will make with the house of Israel after those days, declares the Lord: I will put my law within them, and I will write it on their hearts. And I will be their God, and they shall be my people. And no longer shall each one teach his neighbour and each his brother, saying, 'Know the Lord,' for they shall all know me, from the least of them to the greatest, declares the Lord. For I will forgive their iniquity, and I will remember their sin no more.*

Despite Israel having broken the Mosaic covenant, God promised to make a new, unbreakable covenant with his people. Many in Israel clung to this promise that God would make a new covenant with them, through their darkest days of exile and judgement. The northern kingdom of Israel was conquered by Assyria in 722 BC and destroyed, and then Judah in the south was conquered by Babylon in 586 BC. The people were taken out of their Promised Land into exile in Babylon. Jerusalem was laid waste and the temple destroyed. Seventy years later a remnant of the tribe of Judah returned to Jerusalem where they waited in hope for God to send them their promised Messiah and the new covenant.

About five hundred years later, Jesus the promised Messiah, truly God and truly man, took the Passover meal with his disciples just before he was to be crucified. As they ate the meal, Jesus announced the beginning of the new covenant. He took the bread and wine, saying, "This is my body, which is given for you. Do this in remembrance of me... This cup that is poured out for you is the new covenant in my blood" (Luke 22:19-20). Jesus' arrival on earth, the promised Messiah, the seed of the woman, the offspring of Abraham and David – marked the initiation of the new covenant.[75]

[75] Brown & Keele, *Sacred Bond*, 136-137.

Through this new covenant in Christ, all of God's covenant promises in the Old Testament find their fulfilment. This is why 2 Corinthians 1:20 declares, "For all the promises of God find their Yes in him. That is why it is through him that we utter our Amen to God for his glory."

What is "New" about the New Covenant?

Why do we call the new covenant, "new"? If all of God's people, from all time, are saved through the one covenant of grace, why was it necessary for a new covenant? In essence, it is the coming of Jesus Christ in the fullness of time that is the reason for the "newness" of the new covenant. Christ's coming into the world and his death on the cross and resurrection on the third day marks a profound turning point in redemptive history.

The old covenant, which the New Testament typically associates with the Mosaic covenant (2 Cor. 3:4-14), promised Christ in shadows and types. It was temporary in nature, in that the land of Canaan, the animal sacrifices and various other ceremonial and civil laws were not an end in themselves. Their purpose was to point to a greater reality, a fulfilment of God's promises through the Messiah. The old covenant is thus a shadow of the realities of the gospel, while the new covenant is the substance.[76]

The fulfilment of God's promises under the old covenant is revealed in the new covenant through the shedding of Christ's blood. While the old covenant anticipated the forgiveness of sins through animal sacrifices; in the new covenant sins are effectively dealt with through Christ's one true efficient sacrifice of himself on the cross. He is the true Passover (1 Cor. 5:7), the true Prophet, Priest and King, the true Israel, the true circumcision (Col. 2:11), the true temple of God (Eph. 2:21) and his church, the true seed of Abraham (Gal 3:29). There is therefore nothing of the old covenant that is lost in the new, instead in the new covenant everything is fulfilled and reaches its goal.[77]

The New Covenant brings Blessing

The old covenant required obedience in order to receive God's blessings, "Do this and you will be blessed" (Deut. 28:2). Disobedience would result

[76] Bavinck, *Reformed Dogmatics*, vol. 3, 223.

[77] Bavinck, *Reformed Dogmatics*, vol. 3, 223-224.

in incurring God's curses (Deut. 28:15). The new covenant blesses and saves those who simply trust in what Jesus has already done for them. The old covenant, while certainly pointing to Christ through types and shadows, had no power to produce righteousness or give lasting forgiveness of sins. Instead it revealed that on our own, we are incapable of obeying the law and thus brought condemnation and curse. In the new covenant the curse is broken once and for all by Jesus' death on the cross. Galatians 3:13 tells us that, "Christ redeemed us from the curse of the law by becoming a curse for us." Christians are therefore no longer under any threat of old covenant curses, as Jesus took upon the curse himself. Instead the new covenant offers us gifts and blessings through Jesus, his grace and his righteousness.

The Holy Spirit is poured out under the New Covenant

The Old Testament prophets prophesied that God would pour out his Spirit in abundance in the latter days. In the Old Testament, the Holy Spirit was only poured out on certain prophets, priests and kings. This is why Joel, looking forward to the new covenant realities, prophesies that, "I will pour out my Spirit on all flesh; your sons and your daughters shall prophesy, your old men shall dream dreams, and your young men shall see visions. Even on the male and female servants in those days I will pour out my Spirit" (2:28-29).

Under the new covenant, the Spirit is poured out in greater measure than under the old, enabling all God's people to obey God's law from the heart. While Old Testament saints were most certainly regenerated by the Spirit, they did not experience this greater measure of the outpouring of the Spirit which characterises the new covenant. The coming of the Spirit in the new covenant, initiated at Pentecost, also brought glimpses of heaven to earth. In the new covenant we get to taste of the "powers of the age to come" breaking through into the present age through the Holy Spirit (Heb. 6:5).

The Gentiles are grafted in under the New Covenant

The old covenant was given exclusively to the nation of Israel during its time in the Promised Land. Under the new covenant, God grafted in the Gentiles, the nations of the world, to be included among his people, not just the nation of Israel. The people of God, the church, is now the new Israel, made up of believing Jews and Gentiles (Eph. 2:14). While the nation of Israel under the old covenant was a physical political entity, the new Israel, the church, under the new covenant is spiritual and heavenly.

The New Covenant is Everlasting

The old covenant was temporary, a shadow, only pointing to something much greater (Heb. 8:13, 10:1). It was designed specifically for Israel's dwelling in the Promised Land and was mediated by human beings, Moses and later the various priests who made the sacrifices before God. The new covenant on the other hand is the fulfilment of the old, and is everlasting in nature. It is mediated by Jesus, God himself, our great high priest forever who has made atonement for sins himself. The inheritance of the new covenant is not a physical piece of land, but a heavenly kingdom, the New Jerusalem which is everlasting.[78]

Biblical Evidence for the New Covenant

Jeremiah 31:31-34

This key passage reveals very important things regarding the nature of the new covenant. Under the new covenant, God promises to pour out his Spirit in a greater measure upon his people, compared to the old covenant, empowering them to obey his law from the heart (31:33). All believers in Christ are under the new covenant, and this means that we are all filled with the Holy Spirit who enables us to live lives in obedience to God, for his glory.

It also promised that God would forgive sins, that he would remember them no more (31:34). Under the old covenant, sins had to be atoned for through animal sacrifices each year made by the priests which only removed the guilt of sin temporarily. In the new covenant, Jesus, our Great High Priest, is himself the final and sufficient sacrifice for sins and therefore completely and effectively forgives sin. This is why Hebrews 10:11-12 says, "And every priest stands daily at his service, offering repeatedly the same sacrifices, which can never take away sins. But when Christ had offered for

---

[78] Brown & Keele, *Sacred Bond*, 137-139.

all time a single sacrifice for sins, he sat down at the right hand of God." Jesus' payment of himself for sins, as our perfect High Priest ensures that no more sacrifices for sins ever have to be made. His sacrifice is entirely sufficient to pay for every single sin of all his people for all time.

This passage also looks forward to the new covenant promise of eternal life in the age to come where there would be no more sin, everyone would perfectly know the Lord and God will be our God and we his people (31:33-34).[79]

Ezekiel 36-37

Ezekiel 36:26-27 says, "I will remove the heart of stone from your flesh and give you a heart of flesh. And I will put my Spirit within you, and cause you to walk in my statutes and be careful to obey my rules." This looks forward to the new covenant reality where the Holy Spirit would be poured out on God's people in a greater way than under the old covenant. God's Word and his Spirit work together in bringing new life to dead bones, as chapter 37 goes on to describe. The new covenant will empower God's people to walk in obedience to him, as 37:24 says.[80]

2 Corinthians 3

Paul contrasts the old and new covenants in this passage. The old covenant is described as "the letter which kills" (3:6), while the new covenant is associated with the Spirit who gives life (3:6). The old covenant revealed God's righteousness by the law, it showed up our sin, but it could not provide righteousness to us. This is why Paul calls it, "the ministry of death" (3:7) and the ministry of condemnation (3:9). It required an obedience that no one could ever match up to, and then it condemned those who fell short of it.

What then was the purpose of the old covenant? It was to show our need for Jesus. He fulfilled all the demands of the old covenant, only he has fully obeyed the law. In the new covenant we are counted as righteous before God as our trust is in his obedience, not our own. The Holy Spirit now transforms us inwardly according to the image of Christ – bringing

---

[79] Brown & Keele, *Sacred Bond*, 140-142.

[80] Brown & Keele, *Sacred Bond*, 142-143.

us freedom from the condemnation of the law and from slavery to sin, enabling us to obey God from the heart and beholding his glory in increasing measure (3:17-18).[81]

Covenant Signs and Seals

Covenant signs and seals serve to point to a greater reality signified by the covenant (sign) and bring to effect God's promises and blessings through his covenant (seal). The signs and seals of the new covenant are baptism and the Lord's Supper. Jesus instituted both of these as sacraments, things to be continually observed by his church until he returns. How do baptism and the Lord's Supper act as signs and seals of the new covenant?

Baptism

Baptism is a sign of being incorporated into the new covenant. Under the old covenant, circumcision (painful and bloody) was performed to show that one had entered into the covenant community. Under the new covenant, because Christ's blood has already been spilt, circumcision is no longer necessary. Instead it is baptism (which is painless and blood-less) that is a sign which shows that we are part of the covenant community, the church.[82] When someone makes a profession of faith in Christ or is born into a believing family, they receive the sign of baptism to show that they are now a part of the church. It is a sign that we are united to Christ and belong to him, and seals us with the promises of the gospel. Yet baptism in itself does not save anyone from their sins or regenerate them by the act (this is known as baptismal regeneration, which is taught by Rome) – salvation is through faith in Christ alone.

Baptism is a great picture of our salvation, it is a picture, a visible word, of the blessings of the new covenant. As water washes away dirt, baptism shows how Christ washes away our sins. As rain makes the desert bloom, the rain of God's Spirit poured out on us makes our dead hearts live. Water also drowns things, our old sin nature is drowned and put to death in baptism.[83]

---

[81] Brown & Keele, *Sacred Bond*, 144-145.

[82] Belgic Confession 34.

[83] Belgic Confession 34.

In Christ, under the new covenant, we receive the forgiveness of sins, are united to Christ, given the promise of eternal life in him. Through baptism, God seals these benefits of the new covenant to us.[84]

The Lord's Supper

Under the old covenant, the nation of Israel celebrated the Passover every year to commemorate the Lord's deliverance of them out of slavery in Egypt, and into the Promised Land. In the final plague, God struck down the firstborn of Egypt. To avoid this judgement, Israel was instructed to slaughter a lamb, paint its blood on their doorposts, and then roast and eat the lamb in haste of their departure from Egypt.

In the new covenant, Jesus fulfils the Passover meal as he himself is the Passover Lamb. His blood is shed and his body broken on the cross. Trusting in his sacrifice for sins, covered by his blood, God's wrath passes over us, and instead we are forgiven of our sins and counted as God's own people. Instead of our own blood having to be spilt as penalty for our sins, Christ's blood is spilt. Instead of our own bodies being broken and crushed in judgement, Christ's body is broken for our sake. The Passover meal therefore finds fulfilment in the new covenant in the form of Christ's sacrifice on the cross.[85]

Moments before he went to die on the cross, he instituted the Lord's Supper and said, "This cup that is poured out for you is the new covenant in my blood" (Luke 22:20). As the old covenant was ratified by the pouring out of blood of animals in Exodus 24 and a covenant meal before God's presence (see chapter 4), so the new covenant was ratified by the pouring out of Jesus' blood. Jesus' words of institution (Matt. 26:27-29, Mark 14:23-25, Luke 22:19-20) are direct echoes of Exodus 24:8, "Behold the blood of the covenant that the Lord has made with you in accordance with all these words."

---

[84] Horton, *Introducing Covenant Theology*, 144-155; Thomas, 'Covenant, Assurance, and the Sacraments' 572-577.

[85] Herman Bavinck. *Reformed Dogmatics, vol. 4, Holy Spirit, Church and New Creation,* ed. John Bolt, trans. John Vriend. (Grand Rapids: Baker Academic, 2008), 540-544.

The Supper is therefore a sign of the new covenant: it points to what Jesus did on the cross for us – his blood was shed, and body was broken for our sake, promising us the forgiveness of sins and hope of eternal life. It is also a seal of the new covenant. Every time we partake of it, God renews afresh the benefits and promises of the new covenant to us – we are united to Christ by his Spirit, lifted up into heavenly places before his presence as we feed on him by faith, and assured of our salvation, knowing that one day we will eat and drink with the Lord in the new creation.[86]

The Significance of the New Covenant

It protects us from thinking we have to earn our salvation

Our natural tendency is to work our way up to God through good works, spiritual techniques and practices, acts of mercy or trying harder. The reality which the old covenant shows up is that we are fundamentally unable to produce our own righteousness – we always fail.

What we need instead is a new heart. This only God can give us. He changes our heart of stone to a heart of flesh and he raises us from death to life by the power of the Holy Spirit, which enables us to receive Christ by faith. In the new covenant we rest in Christ's finished work, that he has done everything necessary to restore us to God: he has forgiven our sins, obeyed the law on our behalf, given us the gift of his Spirit, granted us life instead of the death we deserved, and counted his righteousness to us. We receive these incredible gospel benefits, not by working for them, but simply by believing in Christ Jesus.[87]

It causes us to worship God

God's covenant promise that he will be our God and we his people is fulfilled in the new covenant. We get to experience a taste of this reality each Lord's Day when we gather to worship God, where his covenant promises are renewed to us. Every time we worship and gather as the covenant community, we come to Mount Zion, to the city of the living God, the

[86] Westminster Confession of Faith 27.1; Horton, *Introducing Covenant Theology*, 155-163; Thomas, 'Covenant, Assurance, and the Sacraments', 578-580.

[87] Belgic Confession 23; Westminster Confession of Faith 11.1.

heavenly Jerusalem, surrounded by the angels, and get a small glimpse of what is to come in eternity. When we hear God's Word preached and receive the sacraments, the Holy Spirit works powerfully in renewing and strengthening our hearts in grace, conveying to us afresh the blessings and promises of the new covenant.

Conclusion

The beauty of the new covenant is that Jesus has satisfied the demands of the law on our behalf. We do not need to tick off a list of things or perform certain good works in order to get right with God. Jesus has done it all. What then should our only response to this gift of grace be? That we joyfully receive Christ by faith. Repentance and obedient lives that desire to glorify God and enjoy him naturally flow from having received this gift of grace by faith in Christ Jesus.

Philippians 3:8b-9 proclaims, "that I may gain Christ and be found in him, not having a righteousness of my own that comes from the law, but that which comes through faith in Christ, the righteousness from God that depends on faith."

Through faith in Christ we are made right with God forever, our sins are forgiven, we have assurance of our salvation in him and know that nothing can ever separate us from his love. This is why Hebrews 10:23 says, "Let us hold fast the confession of our hope without wavering, for he who promised is faithful." Because of God's faithful promise to us in this new covenant, we relate to him not insecurely or fearfully never knowing where we stand with him, but instead we are absolutely secure in his love for us, as his beloved children, knowing he favours us. We can rest in this eternal hope we have in our God whose promises are faithful and true!

The ultimate promise of the new covenant therefore, is that God's people will dwell with God forever in a new garden – the new creation, the new Jerusalem, the true Promised Land. The curse of sin and death will be finally destroyed and the head of the serpent crushed. There, God will be our God, and we his people forever. Revelation 21:1-4:

> *Then I saw a new heaven and a new earth, for the first heaven and the first earth had passed away, and the sea was no more. And I*

saw the holy city, new Jerusalem, coming down out of heaven from God, prepared as a bride adorned for her husband. And I heard a loud voice from the throne saying, "Behold, the dwelling place of God is with man. He will dwell with them, and they will be his people, and God himself will be with them as their God He will wipe away every tear from their eyes, and death shall be no more, neither shall there be mourning, nor crying, nor pain any more, for the former things have passed away."

Discussion Questions

1. What is new about the new covenant?
2. Explain the connection between the new covenant and the Abrahamic covenant.
3. Explain how the work of the Holy Spirit changes under the new covenant.
4. What is the significance of Jesus' work on the cross in the light of the new covenant promises?
5. Explain how the Lord's Supper is a sign and a seal of the new covenant. Why is it so important for us to partake of the Supper as Christ's church?
6. What is the gospel? How are the promises of the gospel contained in the new covenant?
7. What should our response be to the gospel promises of the new covenant?
8. Overall, how do God's covenant promises to us reveal to us his faithfulness and steadfast love?

Conclusion

Understanding the covenants of Scripture lifts up our eyes to God, the source of these covenants. His covenants reveal something of his character and nature. We are only too familiar with the disappointment of broken promises in this world. In great contrast to this, our God keeps his promises. Through his covenants he shows himself, above all, to be faithful to saving a people for himself.

Though Adam broke the first covenant that God made with him, plunging mankind after him into a sin-cursed existence, God did not forsake his people. He was faithful to the promise he made in Genesis 3:15, where he established a second covenant, to send a seed of Eve to crush the head of the serpent, break the curse and destroy the power of sin. God gradually fulfils this promise through his subsequent covenants with Noah, Abraham, Moses and David. In each, he points increasingly to this promised Champion, Messiah and Divine King that would come and bring the promise to fulfilment.

In the fullness of time, God's promise is fulfilled in the coming of Jesus Christ, truly God and truly man, the seed of the woman. By his perfectly righteous life and atoning death on the cross, he crushed the serpent, Satan, undoing the curse and breaking the power of sin. Through this new covenant, the fulfilment of the covenant of grace, God, through his Son Jesus Christ, rescues us his people from slavery to sin, delivering us from sure judgement that we deserved, forgiving us our sins and raising us up into new, everlasting life with him – all to be received by faith as a gift of grace! Indeed our God is faithful, gracious, merciful, good, holy and loving. In the light of his abundant goodness which we see displayed throughout his covenants with his people, our hearts can only but cry out in the words of Psalm 100:

Make a joyful noise to the Lord, all the earth!
Serve the Lord with gladness!
Come into his presence with singing!

Know that the Lord, he is God!
It is he who made us, and we are his;
we are his people, and the sheep of his pasture.

Enter his gates with thanksgiving,
and his courts with praise!
Give thanks to him; bless his name!

For the Lord is good;
his steadfast love endures for ever,
and his faithfulness to all generations.

Bibliography

Belgic Confession (1561).

Canons of Dort (1619).

Heidelberg Catechism. (1563).

The Westminster Confession of Faith. (1647).

The Westminster Larger Catechism. (1647).

An Anglican Prayer Book, 1989, Church of the Province of Southern Africa, Cape Town: Collins, 1989.

Barth, Karl. *Church Dogmatics, 14 vols.*, eds. G.W. Bromiley and T.F. Torrance, Edinburgh: T & T Clark, 1936-68.

Bavinck, Herman. *Reformed Dogmatics, vol. 2, God and Creation,* ed. John Bolt, trans. John Vriend, Grand Rapids: Baker Academic, 2008.

Bavinck, Herman. *Reformed Dogmatics, vol. 3, Sin and Salvation in Christ,* ed. John Bolt, trans. John Vriend, Grand Rapids: Baker Academic, 2008.

Bavinck, Herman. *Reformed Dogmatics, vol. 4, Holy Spirit, Church and New Creation,* ed. John Bolt, trans. John Vriend, Grand Rapids: Baker Academic, 2008.

Beeke, Joel R. & Jones, Mark, *A Puritan Theology: Doctrine for Life*, Grand Rapids: Reformation Heritage Books, 2012.

Belcher, Richard P. 'The Covenant of Works in the Old Testament' in *Covenant Theology: Biblical, Theological, and Historical Perspectives,* eds. Guy Prentiss Waters, J. Nicholas Reid, and John R. Muether, Wheaton: Crossway, 2020.

Belcher, Richard P. *The Fulfillment of the Promises of God: An explanation of Covenant Theology*, Fearn: Christian Focus Publications, 2020.

Berkhof, Louis. *Systematic Theology*, Edinburgh: Banner of Truth, 1949.

Brown, Michael G. 'The Covenantal Foundation of the Heidelberg Catechism' in *Puritan Reformed Journal* 7, 1, 2015.

Brown, Michael G. & Keele, Zach. *Sacred Bond: Covenant Theology Explored*, San Diego: Reformed Fellowship, 2012.

Calvin, John. *Institutes of the Christian Religion*, trans. Lewis Ford Battles, ed. John T. McNeill, Philadelphia: Westminster John Knox, 1960.

Clowney, Edmund P. *The Unfolding Mystery: Discovering Christ in the Old Testament*, Leicester: Inter-Varsity Press, 1988.

DeYoung, Kevin. 'Afterword: Why Covenant Theology?' in *Covenant Theology: Biblical, Theological, and Historical Perspectives*, eds. Guy Prentiss Waters, J. Nicholas Reid, and John R. Muether, Wheaton: Crossway, 2020.

Duncan, Ligon. 'Covenant in the Early Church' in *Covenant Theology: Biblical, Theological, and Historical Perspectives*, eds. Guy Prentiss Waters, J. Nicholas Reid, and John R. Muether, Wheaton: Crossway, 2020.

Duncan, Ligon. 'Foreword' in *Covenant Theology: Biblical, Theological, and Historical Perspectives*, eds. Guy Prentiss Waters, J. Nicholas Reid, and John R. Muether, Wheaton: Crossway, 2020.

Estelle, Bryan D, Fesko J.V., and VanDrunen, David. 'Introduction' in *The Law is not of Faith: Essays on Works and Grace in the Mosaic Covenant*, eds. Bryan D. Estelle, J.V. Fesko and David VanDrunen, Phillipsburg: P&R Publishing, 2009.

Ferry, Brenton C. 'Works in the Mosaic Covenant: A Reformed Taxonomy' in *The Law is not of Faith: Essays on Works and Grace in the Mosaic Covenant*, eds. Bryan D. Estelle, J.V. Fesko and David VanDrunen, Phillipsburg: P&R Publishing, 2009.

Fesko, J.V. *Adam and the Covenant of Works*, Fearn: Christian Focus Publications, 2021.

Fesko, J.V. *The Theology of the Westminster Standards: Historical Context & Theological Insights*, Wheaton: Crossway, 2014.

Fesko, J.V. *The Trinity and the Covenant of Redemption*, Fearn: Christian Focus Publications, 2016.

Griffith, Howard. 'Covenant in Reformation Theology' in *Covenant Theology: Biblical, Theological, and Historical Perspectives*, eds. Guy Prentiss Waters, J. Nicholas Reid, and John R. Muether, Wheaton: Crossway, 2020.

Horton, Michael. *Introducing Covenant Theology*, Grand Rapids: Baker Books, 2006.

Johnson, Dennis E. *Him We Proclaim, Preaching Christ from All the Scriptures*, Phillipsburg: P&R Publishing, 2007.

Johnson, Dennis E. *Walking with Jesus through His Word: Discovering Christ in All the Scriptures*, Phillipsburg, P&R Publishing, 2015.

Kline, Meredith G. *Kingdom Prologue: Genesis Foundations for a Covenantal Worldview*, Eugene: Wipf & Stock, 2006.

Letham, Robert. *Systematic Theology*, Wheaton: Crossway, 2019.

Poythress, Vern S. *Theophany: A Biblical Theology of God's Appearing*, Wheaton: Crossway, 2018.

Reid, J. Nicholas. 'The Mosaic Covenant' in *Covenant Theology: Biblical, Theological, and Historical Perspectives*, eds. Guy Prentiss Waters, J. Nicholas Reid, and John R. Muether, Wheaton: Crossway, 2020.

Redd, John Scott. 'The Abrahamic Covenant' in *Covenant Theology: Biblical, Theological, and Historical Perspectives*, eds. Guy Prentiss Waters, J. Nicholas Reid, and John R. Muether, Wheaton: Crossway, 2020.

Robertson, O. Palmer. *The Christ of the Covenants*, Phillipsburg: P&R Publishers, 1980.

Thomas, Derek W.H. 'Covenant, Assurance, and the Sacraments' in *Covenant Theology: Biblical, Theological, and Historical Perspectives*, eds. Guy Prentiss Waters, J. Nicholas Reid, and John R. Muether, Wheaton: Crossway, 2020.

Turretin, Francis. *Institutes of Elenctic Theology*, ed. James T. Dennison, Jr., trans. George Musgrave Giger, Philadelphia: P&R Publishing, 1992.

VanDrunen, David. *Living in God's Two Kingdoms: A Biblical Vision for Christianity and Culture*, Wheaton: Crossway, 2010.

VanDrunen, David. *Politics after Christendom: Political Theology in a fractured world*, Grand Rapids: Zondervan, 2020.

Van Pelt, Miles V. 'The Noahic Covenant of the Covenant of Grace' in in *Covenant Theology: Biblical, Theological, and Historical Perspectives*, eds. Guy Prentiss Waters, J. Nicholas Reid, and John R. Muether, Wheaton: Crossway, 2020.

Waters, Guy Prentiss. 'The Covenant of Works in the New Testament' in in *Covenant Theology: Biblical, Theological, and Historical Perspectives*, eds. Guy Prentiss Waters, J. Nicholas Reid, and John R. Muether, Wheaton: Crossway, 2020.

Watson, Thomas. *A Body of Divinity*, Edinburgh: Banner of Truth Trust, 1965.

Woolsey, Andrew A. *Unity and Continuity in Covenantal Thought: A Study in the Reformed Tradition to the Westminster Assembly*, Grand Rapids: Reformation Heritage Books, 2012.

Printed in Great Britain
by Amazon

49321876R00055